CALLED BY A NEW NAME

*You shall be called by a new name...
and your land shall be married.*

cf Is 62:2-4

Evelyn Hosford

Called by a New Name

A Psycho-Spiritual Exploration
of Personal Vocation

ST PAULS

ST PAULS
Morpeth Terrace, London SW1P 1EP, U.K.
Moyglare Road, Maynooth, Co. Kildare, Ireland

ISBN 085439 528 8

Set by TuKan, High Wycombe
Produced in the EC
Printed by The Guernsey Press Co. Ltd., Guernsey, C.I.

ST PAULS is an activity of the priests and brothers
of the Society of St Paul who proclaim the Gospel
through the media of social communication

Dedicated in loving memory to my father,
John Hewitt Hosford (Jack)

Acknowledgements

I am deeply grateful to my second 'family', the Sisters of Charity of St Paul, for the opportunity of hearing Herbert Alphonso S.J. speak about *Personal Vocation*; and for Fr Herbie's gracious permission to use his work. My gratitude also goes to the staff of the Milltown Institute (where the seed of this book was sown), in particular to Brian O'Leary S.J., director of the Graduate Spirituality Programme and author of the Preface to this work; to Jack Finnegan S.D.B. for his inspiring introduction to Jungian psychology and for his guidance through my academic dissertation; and to my friend Brid O'Brien for all her assistance in the Institute's library. A word of thanks also to my brother, Kieran, who typed the original manuscript; and to my friend Margaret Mattison S.P. for her proof-reading skills and suggestions. Last but not least, I express a very special thank you to Mary Clare Dunne S.P. for her friendship, constant support and encouragement to write.

Contents

Part One: Theory

Part Two: Praxis

Preface

Karl Rahner's dictum that the Christian of the future will be a mystic or not exist at all has become something of a cliché. Yet it still speaks very powerfully to many people, reminding them that one of the most significant changes in late-modern culture has been the turn to experience. Post-modern culture further emphasises this turn. We might sum up the implications of Rahner's view in three propositions:

Christianity is no longer a social given.
Each individual has to make a deliberate and free choice to become a disciple of Christ.
This choice will be based on religious experience.

Such religious experience enables us to name the sacred in our lives, to name God in our lives.

An earlier writer, Baron Friedrich von Hugel, distinguished between:

the institutional element in the Church;
the intellectual element in the Church;
the mystical element in the Church.

The institutional and intellectual elements have been highly valued and strongly developed whereas the mystical element has remained the poor relation. This imbalance is the root cause of many of our contemporary problems in the Church. It has produced an inevitable reaction whereby many Christians have opted for discipleship without Church, for spirituality without religion. More positively it has led to a desire to retrieve the rich Christian tradition of spirituality (from East and West) as well as a willingness to bring this tradition into dialogue with other religious traditions and secular disciplines.

Indeed, it can be argued that spirituality, as an object of study and research, is no longer a subdivision of (moral) theology as it had been in the post-Tridentine Church, but is developing into a new autonomous discipline. This new discipline is of its nature *interdisciplinary*. It calls on theology certainly, but it also regards specialities such as psychology, anthropology, sociology, literature, aesthetics and so forth as legitimate and necessary partners. It has broadened the meaning of the word 'spirituality' enormously from its seventeenth century usage as a synonym for the 'devout life'. Consequently, it must be admitted, it has not yet found a commonly agreed and clearly defined focus. But this should not surprise anyone since, in its new contemporary form, the study of spirituality is a discipline still in its infancy.

Psychology was the first of the dialogue partners for theology to be recognized and given acceptance. It could hardly be otherwise. Our way of experiencing and understanding ourselves could never be the same again after Freud. Yet there was, and still is in some circles, a resistance to this dialogue. Extreme positions are taken. Since the Christian life is the effect of grace in us, some argue, there is no place for psychology – grace is all! There is no real difference between human (psychological) and spiritual growth, say others – psychology is all! The first approach demonises Freud (and Jung) while the second canonises them. Somewhere in between lies the truth.

Evelyn Hosford's book, *Called by a New Name*, is a welcome contribution to an open and fruitful dialogue between theology and spirituality. By bringing together the teaching of the Indian Jesuit, Herbert Alphonso, on *personal vocation* and that of the Swiss psychologist, Carl Jung, on *individuation* and the *inner marriage*, she allows each to illuminate the other. Firstly by presenting a theoretical exploration of the issues, and then by offering a series of suggestions that move towards praxis, Hosford challenges the reader intellectually and affectively. She invites us to embark on the journey of life at a deeper level than heretofore and with new energy. I hope that many will take up this invitation with gratitude and courage.

Brian O'Leary S.J.
The Milltown Institute of
Theology and Philosophy, Dublin.

General Introduction

In the Easter of 1992, I had the privilege of meeting Herbert Alphonso S.J., and of hearing him speak about the *Personal Vocation*. I had a deep sense that his message held a profound treasure and that he, himself, was an embodiment of that treasure (cf Mt 13:44-46). He had a quality of radiance which made me think of the divine. I heard his words and my heart knew that he lived and moved and had his being in God. Somewhere deep within me I felt the stirrings of a desire for wholeness and holiness. In a sense the Christ in him spoke at a deep level to the Christ in me. He was a graced person and his intimacy with Christ Jesus created a graced situation.

A year later Jack Finnegan S.D.B. gave me my first serious introduction to Jungian psychology and to the process of Individuation at the Milltown Institute, Dublin. This produced a similar experience and I felt that Jung's message and Alphonso's message had many similarities, but that one was from the standpoint of depth psychology and the other from the viewpoint of Christian spirituality. Since both authors advocate integration, and since their words reverberated deep within me, I was drawn to attempt a synthesis of *Personal Vocation* and the process of Individuation, which leads to the discovery of one's personal myth.

Adrian Cunningham points out that, "Theologians remain divided about whether Jung has provided fresh evidence for the *anima naturaliter christiana* thesis or whether he has erected an aesthetically beguiling alternative to Christianity."[1] Whatever the theological truth may be, Carl Jung's analytical psychology offers an important, indeed vital, challenge to every theologian to make experience an integral part of his or her theologizing. Personally, I agree with those individuals who hold that Jung's psychology has "liberating possibilities for renewal of faith".[2]

15

In an age possessed by the rational mind, Jung may be hailed as a prophet who has restored the value of myth to consciousness and who has opened the way, once again, for Dionysian irrationality and intuition to lead us beyond the ego to ecstatic union. However, it is important not to be uncritical of Jung's theory and to realize that it does hold a certain threat for traditional Western religiosity. Unfortunately, a criticism of Jung's theory is beyond the scope of this book and I am aware that many issues are not dealt with adequately. The aim of this work is a simple synthesis in an effort to re-embody and to renew the traditional Christian myth.

In this postmodern world, with its experience of chaos and fragmentation, I believe that a synthesis of Jung's *Personal Myth* and Alphonso's *Personal Vocation* holds one key to a sense of unity and integration. Our days are also experiencing the gathering momentum of "New Age" spiritualities. While much is to be commended in New Age spiritualities, there is also an attempt to replace the old Christian myth which is failing to bring a sense of purpose and meaning to the lives of many people. Instead of discarding the old Christian myth for a completely new and alternative one, I believe we can rediscover the old myth in a deeply personal and unique way. Through a synthesis of *Personal Myth* and *Personal Vocation*, we remain firmly rooted in history and grounded in tradition. At the same time, we experience the freshness and depth of our own unique and personal experience.

The discovery of our *personal myth* and *personal vocation* has the power to fill the yawning gulf of meaninglessness. The discovery of our unique divine spark holds, in potential, the living flame of love; holds, in potential, the moments of ecstatic joy and mystical union which so many hearts desire. Our *personal myth* and *personal vocation* are that sacred space of inner marriage and spiritual union; that sacred space which empowers us to have being in the world and to enter into relationship with the Ground of all Being.

This synthesis is directed primarily to Christians: Christians of every denomination and none. It is also written for anybody with an interest in the relationship between psychology and spirituality, and particularly for those with an interest in psycho-spiritual development from a Jungian perspective.

One of the aims of the synthesis is to broaden the understanding of vocation. The word "vocation" has been used – notably in Roman Catholic circles – in an elitist sense for far too long. The impression has been given that only the clergy and those in the various forms of Religious Life have a vocation. Vocation is not the prerogative of a few. Each individual has a vocation. God calls each individual by name and, in doing so, binds the individual to God's very own self. The word "religion" comes from the Latin *religare* which means "to bind". In its most radical sense every individual lives a religious life since every individual is bound to God: the Ground and Source of all Being.

In a similar vein, this synthesis is written with the belief that the heights and depths of mysticism are not reserved for the celibate monk or nun. All may be graced by mystical experience.

It is the mystical experience of the numinous which depth psychologist, Carl G. Jung, found to be most healing for the individual. The inner, mystical marriage of the masculine and the feminine, which gives birth to the Self, is the symbol of wholeness and of the divine-human encounter. Jung believed that there was a basic drive in the human psyche toward wholeness and meaning. This basic drive is the process of Individuation which unfolds one's personal myth and personal meaning in life.

Even though the symbolism of mystical marriage, or bridal imagery, does not surface in Ignatian spirituality, Ignatius' goal is an integrated life in union with God. Alphonso firmly believes that the discernment of our *personal vocation*, which is written into our concrete history, holds the secret of unity and meaning at the heart of life; and he describes it as an interpersonal love relationship.

17

Both Jung and Alphonso realize the profound relationship between personal meaning and wholeness or integration. Therefore this synthesis is written for anybody who is faced with a crisis of meaning; for the individual searching for a deeper identity; for anybody who longs for a sense of unity and integration amid the fragmentation and brokenness of life.

Additionally, it is an attempt to contextualize and ground Western Christian spirituality. Unfortunately, the "body" and the "world" have suffered bad press in Western Christian spirituality down through the centuries. Christian spirituality, in the West, has yet to fully grasp that the journey into the realm of spirit is also a body-soul experience lived out in this world. Jung's depth psychology helps to contextualize the realm of spirit which Herbert Alphonso discusses in his concept of *personal vocation*.

Alphonso tells the story of a middle-aged Jesuit to illustrate what he means by an individual's *personal vocation*. This middle-aged Jesuit shared with Alphonso his feelings of negligence in prayer. In an effort to help him, Alphonso asked if he ever felt spontaneously close to, or in union with, God. Immediately the man started talking about the goodness of God with a depth of life and energy. The goodness of God, this man discovered, was the secret of his prayer, of all his relationships, of his work and of his leisure-time. Looking back over his life, it was written into his concrete history. In a deeply personal and unique way these words summed up his life and very being. It was his personal myth summarized in four words. So, this synthesis is for anybody who wants to get in touch with his or her own story.

The first part of the synthesis is a more theoretical exploration of *Personal Vocation, Personal Myth* and the *Inner Marriage.* A brief exploration of the power of word and name, coupled with the biblical vision of transformative call, forms a background to Alphonso's *Personal Vocation.* The motifs of danger, risk and woundedness which surface from this background exploration are not examined by Alphonso, but they are complemented by Jung's psychological perspective of vocation. The experience of vocation takes us to the edges of consciousness, to unexpected places, to the margins of life. We are wounded by the crowd and wounded by the wilderness, but it is through our woundedness as human beings that divine life ultimately flows. It is through our woundedness and suffering that we hear the invitation to the Inner Marriage. It is through our woundedness that we cleave to our Lover and are healed and made whole. It is through our woundedness that we drink the wine of ecstasy.

The second part of the synthesis offers some practical suggestions and exercises for *Sabbath time*. *Sabbath time* is sacred space when we try to listen to our deepest Centre. The suggestions and exercises offered are possible, but not prescriptive, aids to the discovery and concrete unfolding of our incomparable, God-given uniqueness.

Chapter 9 introduces the possibility of pen-walking and of pattern-noting across the pages of a journal. Ira Progoff's *Intensive Journal* method gives our core creative Self the space to express itself, and we can begin to note our psychic DNA as it unfolds into consciousness.

Chapter 10 briefly explores Jungian Typology and the functions in consciousness. It describes how individuals have a preferred way of functioning and of adapting to reality which gives rise to a dominant and an inferior function. The inferior function lies in the unconscious and is both our stumbling block in every day living and our graced God-connection. The Myers-Briggs Test and the Examination of Consciousness are two suggested ways of discovering our particular psychological type.

Chapter 11 suggests ways to encourage our unconscious identity to reveal itself in dream symbols and imagery. Dreams are Godspeak and channels of divine revelation. They wound our consciousness with the realization that there is a greater Reality beyond our ego-centric world. As symbols rise from our deeper Centre, our personal myth with its God-given meaning in life unfolds. This unfolding may be stretched through active imagination and imaginative contemplation.

Lectio Divina or divine, sacred reading is introduced in chapter 12 as a time-honoured method of meditative reading. This meditative reading vibrates and echoes within us as individuals, helping us to get in touch with the core of our being. The mystery of the word in Scripture speaks to the mystery of the word in our very depths and becomes an integrative part of our lives.

Chapter 13 gives a brief background, from a Jungian perspective, to the Ignatian Spiritual Exercises which Alphonso describes as the privileged way of discerning our *personal vocation*. It also outlines some practical points and suggestions.

Chapter 14 presents a number of short, reflective exercises the simplicity of which can tap into the depths of our *personal vocation* and personal myth.

The last chapter, The Power of Logos and Eros, echoes the first, and it develops the masculine and feminine principles inherent in word and name. The word, or logos, is the differentiating masculine principle while personal naming is the feminine bonding principle. We are made in the image and likeness of God who transcends gender, but is a dynamic movement of masculine and feminine energies. This is the God who calls us by name to the inner marriage of the masculine and the feminine, and to the ongoing birth of the Self.

> This, then, is what I pray, kneeling before the Father and *Mother*, from whom every family, whether spiritual or natural takes its name: Out of *God's* infinite glory, may *God* give you the power through *God's* Spirit for your hidden self to grow strong, so that Christ may live in your hearts through faith, and then planted in love and built on love, you will with all the saints

have strength to grasp the breadth and the length, the height and the depth; until, knowing the love of Christ, which is beyond all knowledge, you are filled with the utter fullness of God.[3]

NOTES

1   Adrian Cunningham, Jungian Psychology: Its Contribution to Spirituality in A. Richardson & J. Bowden, eds., *A New Dictionary of Christian Theology* (London: SCM Press, 1983) 312-314 at 312. The Latin in this quotation refers to the thesis that the soul is naturally Christian.
2   ibid 312.
3   Ephesians 3:14–19, JB trans. with slight adaptation marked by italics.

Part One

Theory

Chapter 1

The Power of Word and Name

Words stand between silence and silence:
between the silence of things and the silence
of our own being.
Thomas Merton, *Thoughts in Solitude*

Words... Silence... Being. The above quotation from the modern-day mystic, Thomas Merton, conveys a profound relationship between words, silence and our very being. A profound relationship between silence and the word begets meaning and it restores to the word its original power. One of the great famines in modern society is the lack of silence. In this famine, words are bandied about glibly without depth of relatedness and reflection. When words swallow silence they destroy their own meaning and power. Meaning and power are necessary for a deep sense of well-being; they are essential nutrients for the human person.

Novelist, Ursula Le Guin, recognizes this profound relationship and in her fantasy novel, *A Wizard of Earthsea*, she captures the power of silence and the power of the word. The long, listening silence of magi fills this fantasy world and when the magi speak about the simple things of life, it is as if they have just invented speech. The key to this power and meaning, "...has its roots in the Old Speech, that language in which things are named with their true names."[1] The learning of true names is synonymous with knowing the being of a person or thing. It is a powerful gift born in the crucible of silence.

It is possible, too, to have a silence which is unproductive: a "stony" silence which does not protect and nourish the life and meaning of the word; a "stony" silence which blocks real growth. Words are something alive and active:

they have a shape, a bite, a taste, a colour. Words have a power reaching far beyond their dictionary meaning: they can evoke feelings and emotions; they have an associative power which can trigger a chain reaction of thoughts and images in our minds; they can act like echoes bouncing off and releasing our stored-up experiences. Words need space to develop and deepen. They need a silent, listening space... a wise, nurturing and gentle heart.

Words are active at both the conscious and unconscious level of the psyche. The psychoanalyst Jacques Lacan speaks of the Symbolic Order which is constituted by language and its laws. "Symbols", he states, "in fact envelop the life of man in a network so total that they join together, before he comes into the world; they bring to his birth... the shape of his destiny..."[2] The Symbolic Order which is embodied in culture, surrounds the human embryo in the womb. We enter this world with a symbolic-verbal ancestral baggage. While the baby is still in the womb, the external voices of the family circle are already shaping the child's experience and the child's future. The baby not only inherits a family history with its open and hidden chapters, but a national and universal one as well. Words echo throughout the nation shaping the individual's sense of self at both the conscious and unconscious level of the psyche. And words vibrate far beyond national boundaries: they dance, they sing, they cry, they stumble, they die and they rise in universal mythology. Some of these stories have come down to us through the ages and others are but faint echoes buried in our collective unconscious.

The word in story or in narrative form is extremely powerful. As story-teller William J. Bausch states: "A person without a story is a person with amnesia. A country without its story has ceased to exist. A humanity without its story has lost its soul."[3] Story offers us a sense of identity at both the personal and collective levels: we are rooted in a family story; in national history and tradition; in local and universal mythology. Story helps us to remember and to make present: since story belongs to time and is outside time, through story we can visit the past and break out of time's linear dimension. In addition, revisiting the past in narrative form helps us to find a pattern and a shape in our lives and this offers a certain amount of security and control in the midst of chaos and fragmentation. Story is therapeutic: in trying to put narrative order on our lives, we learn to contain personal experiences. Verbalizing our pain and traumas helps us to bear them more easily. Words can create a new skin to cover old and weeping wounds.

If the human words of family, friends, foes and nations are so powerful, then how much more potent is the word of God; how much more powerful is God's word in shaping the life and destiny of the individual.

From the perspective of Christian mythology, the "Old Speech", in Le Guin's fantasy world, is none other than God. It is the Word who was with God in the beginning and through whom all things came to be (cf Jn 1). In the words of St John of the Cross:

> The Father spoke one Word,
> which was his Son, and this Word
> He always speaks in eternal silence,
> and in silence must it be heard by the soul.[4]

God, the source of all being, does not pour out useless words. God's one and only word is the source of all life and meaning. "Our destiny", as Adrian van Kaam notes, "is contained in Christ, for we are contained in him as little words in the Eternal Word. Our deepest self is hidden in Christ and Christ is hidden in God."[5] Christ's story is our story: when God speaks God's one pregnant Word, She-He speaks each one of us for all eternity. It is a powerful Word spoken in love and wisdom.

Long before the dawn of New Testament times, the Jewish people recognized the power of God's word. In the Book of Wisdom we get an energetic image of God's word leaping down from the royal throne:

For while gentle silence
    enveloped all things,
and night in its swift course was
    now half gone,
your all-powerful word leaped
    from heaven, from the
    royal throne,
into the midst of the land that
    was doomed,
 a stern warrior
carrying the sharp sword of your
    authentic command... (Ws 18:14-16).

This image is taken up in the New Testament's Letter to the Hebrews:

Indeed, the word of God is living and active, sharper than any two-edged sword, piercing until it divides soul from spirit, joints from marrow; it is able to judge the thoughts and intentions of the heart. And before him no creature is hidden, but all are naked and laid bare to the eyes of the one to whom we must render an account (Heb 4:12,13).

In the Old Testament the word is called *dabar* and it is impregnated with power and compulsion. Hurled (cf Is 9:8), or gently spoken, Yahweh's word greatly influences the course of history. It can effect both a blessing and a curse.

Dabar is both an operative agent and a creative agent. The prologue to St John's Gospel echoes the creative word of Yahweh in Genesis 1:

In the beginning was the Word, and the Word was with God, and the Word was God. He was in the beginning with God. All things came into being through him, and without him not one thing came into being (Jn 1:1-3).

With the dawn of New Testament times, the word of Yahweh operates in history in a new and definitive way, bringing about a new creation:

> And the Word became flesh and lived among us, and we have seen his glory, the glory of a father's only son, full of grace and truth (Jn 1:14).

This same Word calls us by name into being. This same Word surrounds the embryo in the womb from the very beginning:

> I have called you by name, you are mine (Is 43:1c).

> Before I formed you in the womb I knew you,
> and before you were born I consecrated you...
> (Jer 1:5).

We are born of this very same Word:

> For it was you who formed my inward parts;
> you knit me together in my mother's womb
> (Ps 139:13).

And this same Word calls us into an ongoing birthing process:

> You have been born anew, not of perishable but of imperishable seed, through the living and enduring word of God (1 Pet 1:23).

This is the word which grows and bears fruit in the deep, rich soil of the heart (cf Lk 8:15); the word which does not want us to become strangers to the deepest part of ourselves. This is the word which names us in the silent depth of our being.

In Le Guin's novel, *A Wizard of Earthsea*, the main

character has three names. As a child he bore the name "Duny" which was given him by his mother. Later on, the other children called him "Sparrowhawk" and this he kept throughout life as his use-name. At the age of thirteen, however, he received his true-name or his being-name from his master Ogion in a ritual which echoes Christian baptism. As Sparrowhawk walked through the icy, living water to the far bank, Ogion reached out his hand and whispered his true name: "Ged". As the narrator explains, nobody knows a person's true name except the person and the person's namer, and those to whom one chooses to reveal it. The custom of having different names is not alien to our culture. Each one of us has a family-given name; many of us are aware of having nicknames or pet names, and most of us choose to reveal our being-name i.e. our deepest and truest self, to only a few. The latter is so because the person who knows another's true name holds that other in his or her keeping.

In a fleeting mystical moment, Ged catches a glimpse of his deeper reality when it seemed to him that he was a word spoken by the sunlight. In this mystical moment, "Ged understood the singing of the bird, and the language of the water falling in the basin of the fountain, and the shape of the clouds, and the beginning and end of the wind that stirred the leaves..."[6] Each one of us is a word spoken in the sunlight and by the Sonlight. The Word, the true light (cf Jn 1:9), is our Namer whispering our true name in the silent depths of our hearts. All of creation emanates from and unites in the Word, and every story weaves back to this one universal and eternal Word.

Summary

Words... Silence... Being. In the fertile and silent ground of the heart words rise and fall, powerfully shaping the identity and destiny of each individual. Moving at the very centre of these words is a special word singing us into being; a special word calling us into the depths of who we really are; a special word which is our true-name, our being-name, our God-given name.

We are called by name.

NOTES

1 Ursula Le Guin, *A Wizard of Earthsea* (Middlesex: Penguin/Puffin Books Ltd., (1971) 1986) 30.
2 Jacques Lacan, *Écrits*, trans. by A. Sheridan (London: Routledge, 1992) 68
3 William J. Bausch, *Storytelling, Imagination and Faith* (Mystic, Connecticut: Twenty-Third Pub., (1984) 1988) 33.
4 K. Kavanaugh & O. Rodriguez, eds., *The Collected Works of St John of the Cross* (Washington: ICS Pub., 1979) 675, Maxim 21.
5 Adrian van Kaam, *The Woman at the Well*, (New Jersey: Dimension Books, 1976) 78.
6 Ursula Le Guin, op. cit., 47.

Chapter 2

Called by Name

I will go before you
and level the mountains,...
I will give you the treasures of darkness
and riches hidden in secret places,
so that you may know that it is
I, the Lord,
the God of Israel, who call
you by your name.

Isaiah 45:2a,3

The theme of true names which weaves through Le Guin's novel is also a common biblical motif. In Old Testament thought "name" is often synonymous with "person" or "self". It is not a mere label but is bound up with existence and expresses the essence of personality. A change of name indicates a profound change in the person. In the New Testament, name is also linked with personality. When biblical characters are called by Yahweh or by Jesus their true Self is being awakened.

The Old Testament Vision of Transformative Call

Abraham
Salvation history begins with God's call to Abraham (cf Gen 12). Abraham's story presents the foundational image of call and, from this point on, *Called by Name* is a fundamental motif running through the Bible. The outer journey to the promised land, which takes Abraham from his homeland of Haran, mirrors the inner journey to his deepest Centre. This interior landscape is reflected in the outer plains and

mountainous district (cf Gen 12:8), in the time of famine (cf Gen 12:10), and in the image of spaciousness (cf Gen 13:14,15). Abraham is compelled by the voice of God calling him. It is this voice from his deeper Centre which gives him the strength to face all obstacles in his path; to carry on despite adverse authority; and to survive times of sparse resources. The call of God, wherever it leads our footsteps, is always a call to be our authentic selves. This is the sharp sword of God's authentic command (cf Ws 18:16). The account we must render (cf Heb 4:13) is the story of how we have been our true selves. Abraham's view of the promised land, from east to west, north to south, mirrors his vision of his own interior land. This is why Yahweh called him by the new name of "Abraham".[1] The covenant with Yahweh reveals to Abraham the four dimensions of his true Self, and he enters into a conscious relationship with a Greater Power (cf Gen 17:1-8).

Through the covenant with Yahweh, Abraham comes to experience God's favour and blessing. However, responding to Yahweh's call involves an element of danger and risk. In Abraham's case he is faced with the sacrifice of his son Isaac; and non-biblical legend relates how Abraham had to move to Canaan because his own life was in danger from King Nimrod. Edward F. Edinger points out this ambiguous and dangerous aspect to vocation which can be overlooked. Response to the deep inner call may require the denial of external and projected authority, thus exposing oneself to dangerous reprisal.[2]

Jacob

Genesis 32:23 records Jacob's transformative encounter with God, symbolized by a blessing and the new name of "Israel". As a result of this encounter, the deceitful Jacob becomes father of the chosen people with a new sense of meaning and purpose. However, the blessing and transformation come after a long struggle in the silent darkness of the night, and not without a wounding. Jacob is both blessed and wounded. He experiences darkness and light, strength and weakness before entering the promised land of Canaan. Jacob names the place Peniel which means "face of God". This symbolizes Jacob's glimpse of his own inner, hallowed ground; his own divine Centre where God dwells.

Moses
The theme of holy ground surfaces more explicitly in the call of Moses. Out of reverence, Moses is commanded to remove his sandals and to stand bare-footed before Yahweh. Moses' removal of his sandals is highly symbolic. The journey to his inner Self demands an uncovering and, before entering God's presence, he must co-operate by removing certain obstacles which lie in his path. The first is his obstinate reluctance which kindles the anger of the Lord (cf Ex 4:14), to the point where Yahweh tried to kill him (cf Ex 4:24). Entry into sacred ground is fraught with dangers which play a part in the liberating and transformative process. Moses' life is spared through an act of circumcision: an act which symbolizes acquiescence to the divine will and the recognition of the circumcised as a covenant partner. Moses, too, has the experience of being known by name and of winning God's favour (cf Ex 33:13).

Samuel
Yahweh's persistence is seen in the call of Samuel. This story illustrates how individuals project their inner call onto an outer authority figure (cf 1 Sam 3:2-21). Sometimes this projection is at the expense of a deeply personal relationship with God. Fortunately for Samuel, his authority figure, Eli, had the wisdom to help him listen to his personal call from God, and to enter into his own personal truth.

Judith
Judith was a woman who had a personal relationship with God and relied on her own inner authority. With the Lord's blessing and strength, she answered the call to deliver

the Jewish nation, the promised land, from the oppressive hands of Holofernes. Her plan of deliverance meant, however, that she would have to enter the tent of the oppressor, risk being violated by him and risk losing her virtue (cf Jd 12:16).

Esther

In the story of Esther, Jews of the Diaspora are facing extermination because of their nonconformity. Esther, the Jewish queen of Ahasuerus, risks her own life in responding to the call to deliver her people from this dreadful fate. After prayer and fasting, Esther disobeys the law and approaches the king in the inner court without being summoned: an act which carries the penalty of death. Ahasuerus rises from the throne, his face blazing with anger, but God changes his heart and he reaches out with his golden sceptre to accept Esther, and to revoke the destructive plot against the Jews.

Jeremiah

The prophet Jeremiah was convinced that he was personally called by name (cf Jer 15:16). This conviction empowered Jeremiah to continue with his God-given purpose and mission in life. This he did in the face of all opposition, ridicule and murderous plots. Jeremiah asserted the principle of individual responsibility and he stood out against the collective, but not without paying a price and not without hinting to Yahweh that he was a bully! Jeremiah's struggle and bold arguments with Yahweh illustrate that the call is a vital and dynamic process.

Isaiah

The theme of being called by name is beautifully expressed in Isaiah:

> Do not fear, for I have redeemed you;
> I have called you by name,
> you are mine (Is 43:1).

For the Hebrews, as Fran Ferder points out, "Naming something meant establishing a relationship with that which is named. Once named, the person or thing could not be discarded; it was owned."[3] This relationship does not exclude the danger of being drowned or burned, but faith in, and trusting co-operation with, Yahweh provide ultimate protection (cf Is 43:2). In the Book of Isaiah being called by a new name also brings the blessing of marriage:

> The nations shall see your vindication,
> and all the kings your glory;
> and you shall be called by a new name
> that the mouth of the Lord will give.
>
> You shall be a crown of beauty
>   in the hand of the Lord,
> and a royal diadem in the hand of your God.
>
> You shall no more be termed Forsaken,
> and your land shall no more be termed Desolate;
> but you shall be called My Delight Is in Her,
> and your land Married;
> for the Lord delights in you,
>   and your land shall be married (Is 62:2-4).

Word and Marriage

The word of God has a purpose and a mission which may be summed up in the land having its marriage or wedding. The word of God is alive and active until it has accomplished this mission:

> For as the rain and the snow
>   come down from heaven,
> and do not return there until
>   they have watered the earth,
> making it bring forth and sprout,

giving seed to the sower and bread to the eater,
so shall my word be that goes out from my mouth;
it shall not return to me empty,
but it shall accomplish that which I purpose,
and succeed in the thing for which I sent it

(Is 55:10,11).

The word of God receives its fullest incarnation in the person of Jesus Christ who is the imprint of God's very being (cf Heb 1:1-3). This is the wedding of all weddings: the marriage of God's divine nature with human nature. This is the marriage which takes back the human story – my story and your story – to the heart of the Godhead (cf Jn 1:18).

The New Testament Vision of Transformative Call

The New Testament call of Mary and the disciples is paradigmatic of our call in Christ. In Luke's infancy narrative, the angel acknowledges Mary's family-given name, but in the opening salutation the angel greets her with her God-given name. "Favoured One" is Mary's deepest identity, her truest Self, as the chosen mother of the Messiah: it sums up her whole life. However, her personal call as "Favoured" or "Graced" One would involve the piercing of her own soul by a sword. The sword may symbolize the pain and sorrow involved in responding to a vocation which would lead her to a crucifixion. Jesus' crucifixion is also her crucifixion. Mary's personal vocation and response was a dynamic process. She pondered and treasured things in her heart. She struggled to understand.

Jesus calls Simon son of Jonah by the new name of "Peter" which means "Rock". Even though Peter was "Rock", he had to learn his deepest identity through the process of denial, awareness, acceptance and empathy. Peter's denial of Jesus is a denial of Peter's own truth, a denial of his deepest Self. This denial of his inner truth is a paradigm for all of us. Fortunately, Peter had the courage to face his betrayal; to grow in awareness and acceptance; and to be reconciled with Jesus and with the Way, the Truth and the Life. Judas, on the other hand, betrayed his true Self with a false kiss and failed to enter that demanding process of awareness and acceptance which is life-giving.

The call of Jesus involves the pain of discipleship: the renunciation of self at one level to find the Self at a deeper level. This renunciation is akin to death itself and, if acted out, can result in actual death as in the case of Judas. This death at a psycho-spiritual level, however, has the reward of a rich harvest and a more spacious life. In John's gospel, Jesus the Good Shepherd knows his sheep and calls each one by name. He calls them into rich and spacious pasture-land so that they may have life and have it abundantly (cf Jn 10:3,10).

In Luke's gospel, Jesus exhorts his disciples to rejoice because their names are written in heaven; and in the Book of Revelation we read:

> To everyone who conquers I will give some of the hidden manna, and I will give a white stone, and on the white stone is written a new name that no one knows except the one who receives it (Rev 2:17).

The person who conquers falseness, the person who struggles to be real with self and God, will discover his or her true identity and be called by a new name.

The engraved white stone is given to the individual when he or she has experienced the struggle and process of life's journey. In other words, one has to grow into one's deepest identity; one has to enflesh and become one's God-given name. This name communicates how God sees the individual and it expresses the essence of his or her personality and meaning in life.

The image of stone has a number of cross-references and sacred stones enjoy great significance in various traditions. In the Christian tradition Christ becomes the chief cornerstone: the precious stone which was rejected by the builders (cf Ps 118; Mk 12:10). He is the cornerstone from which we are hewn (cf Is 51:1). Gerard Manley Hopkins echoes the biblical white stone, and he captures the paradox of being valuable and worthless; the paradox of acceptance and rejection; the paradox of multifaceted wholeness:

> ...In a flash, at a trumpet crash,
> I am all at once what Christ is, since he was what
>   I am, and
> This Jack, joke, poor potsherd, patch, matchwood,
>   immortal diamond,
>   Is immortal diamond.
>
> 'That Nature is a Heraclitean Fire'

Summary

Called by Name is a fundamental motif which weaves through the Old and New Testaments. For the Hebrews being named and naming is of deep significance. Being named is bound up with existence itself: without a name one simply does not exist and the name expresses the essence of the person. A change of name indicates a profound transformation and when biblical characters are called by Yahweh or by Jesus their true Self is being awakened. The call from God to be one's deepest and truest Self is a loving call but it is not without elements of danger and risk. Entry into sacred ground is fraught with dangers which play a part in the transformative process. To receive the white stone - to become the immortal diamond - we must risk reprisal and rejection; we must wrestle with the word of God in the darkness and encounter our own woundedness and brokenness. Then the poor potsherd realises that it is, indeed, an immortal diamond.

NOTES

1 Cf Eugene H. Maly, 'Genesis' in R.E. Brown et al, eds., *The Jerome Biblical Commentary* (London: Geoffrey Chapman, 1970) 7-46 at 18 & 20.

2 Cf Edward F. Edinger, *The Bible and the Psyche* (Toronto: Inner City Books, 1986) 26/27.

3 Fran Ferder, *Words Made Flesh: Scripture, Psychology and Human Communication* (Notre Dame, Indiana: Ave Maria Press, 1986) 63.

Chapter 3

Personal vocation: Called in Christ

...In a flash, at a trumpet crash,
I am all at once what Christ is...
  Hopkins, 'That Nature is a Heraclitean Fire'

In his publication, *The Personal Vocation*, Herbert Alphonso S.J. explores the theme of our call and identity in Christ. Alphonso's vision of the transformative call is rooted in the biblical theme Called by Name. While he does not explore the biblical theme, he succinctly summarizes it as saying: I am not one in a crowd for God.[1]

Christ's Unique Mediation

Alphonso points out that, objectively speaking, all calls come from God in the person of Jesus Christ, i.e. the Word made flesh. Alphonso's use of the words "objectively speaking" is very important. The fact that a large number of people do not subjectively acknowledge Jesus as the Christ does not withdraw God's word from creation and it does not limit God's eyesight. God can still discern the multi-faceted expression of God's one Word which holds all meaning.

Alphonso sees Christ's unique mediation between God and humankind in the theme of being uniquely called and named in Christ Jesus. He states:

...all vocations are in Christ Jesus: the personality of Christ Jesus is so infinitely rich that it embraces all calls and vocations. If then each one of us has a "*personal vocation*", this can only be in Christ Jesus.

This means that there is a facet of the personality of Christ Jesus, a "face" of Christ Jesus, which is proper to each one of us...[2]

In other words, there is a unique expression of the Word for me and a unique expression of the Word for you. This unique expression is our God-given name, our deepest identity, our *personal vocation*.

Personal Vocation – Unique Spirit

Alphonso stresses that our *personal vocation* is not on the same level as other hierarchically structured vocations. It is prior to any other vocation and is the spirit which gifts with uniqueness and animates the individual regardless of role in society or hierarchical vocation. In other words, it is an identity deeper than personae and ego-identity.

In fact, Alphonso states that our *personal vocation* "is the person of Christ Jesus himself in a deeply unique way."[3] In 1 Corinthians 6:15-20, St Paul implies that Christ and the Christian share a marriage union which is mysteriously one flesh and one Spirit. Alphonso expresses this mysterious spousal character when he describes *personal vocation* as the person of Christ himself, and as a profoundly interpersonal love relationship between Christ and the individual. Even though the symbolic language of betrothal does not surface in Ignatian spirituality, it is hinted at in Alphonso's description of *personal vocation* and the symbol of marriage lies behind the theme of call and covenant.

Experience of Grace

Alphonso describes the discernment of his *personal vocation* as the single greatest grace of his life. He discovered his integrating "face" of Christ Jesus which touches and shapes his entire being, and which touches and shapes his relationships with others and the world.

In his book, *Reaching Out*, Henri J.M. Nouwen movingly describes a graced moment in the lives of two people; a moment which brought the awareness that we walk on holy ground because Christ touches it in and through us:

> It seemed that while the silence grew deeper around us we became more and more aware of a presence embracing both of us. Then he said, "It is good to be here", and I said, "Yes, it is good to be together again", and after that we were silent again for a long period. And as a deep peace filled the empty space between us he said hesitantly, "When I look at you it is as if I am in the presence of Christ." I did not feel startled, surprised or in need of protesting, but I could only say, "It is the Christ in you, who recognises the Christ in me." "Yes", he said, "He indeed is in our midst"; and then he spoke the words which entered my soul as the most healing words I had heard in many years, "From now on, wherever you go, or wherever I go, all the ground between us will be holy ground."[4]

Grace is not a substance divorced from God, it is an experience of God. It is God lovingly and freely giving of God's self. God's self-communication had one unique moment in history when the Word became flesh and lived among us. This same Word wants to incarnate in the individual in a unique way and to reach out to others. In the depths of our being there is holy ground and Christ still walks the earth.

Our *personal vocation* is an intimate, unique encounter with God in Christ Jesus and grace, as Leonardo Boff notes, is essentially encounter and relationship. The *personal vocation* is an encounter unique to the individual but it has a ripple effect on others and the world. As individuals, we help to shape the history of the world according to our response to or rejection of God's call. If we harden our hearts to our *personal vocation*, we will collude with the oppressive, life-threatening structures in our society; but if we open our hearts to the transformative word of God, we will be a liberating presence. The grace of *personal vocation* is not meant for the individual in an exclusive sense. In Abraham's story, his personal call was also a gift for his descendants; and in Moses' experience it was a liberating gift for the Israelites held captive in Egypt. When we are loyal to our own unique space and try to live out the deepest truth of our being, it has a liberating effect on others. "Grace", Bill Huebsch states, "...is when God communicates God-self to us by revealing us to ourselves."[5] This revelation brings the grace of communion: we are radically alone as individuals yet in relationship with others and the whole cosmos.

In the Genesis story of Adam and Eve, God created the human body intending it to be naked and unclothed. Clothing comes as a result of Adam and Eve's sin. God now calls each one of us to stand naked before God again; to stand in our own naked truth and to allow Jesus to cover us; to allow our *personal vocation* to embrace us; to put on our deepest and truest Self. Grace is that encounter which empowers us to come home to our deepest selves. This journey homeward to ourselves involves an acceptance of ourselves and of our real experience. It also entails holding opposites in creative tension. Our ability to do so rests on Christ's having first accepted us by name and having shared fully in our humanity.

Personal Meaning

Influenced by Victor Frankl and his school of therapy known as Logotherapy, Alphonso realizes the vital importance of personal meaning. During his time at the concentration camp at Auschwitz, Frankl noted what was meaningful in the life stories of other prisoners. When Frankl fed back meaning to these prisoners he observed that they were revitalized and they regained the will to live. Alphonso takes this idea a step further and he distinguishes between many possible man-given meanings and the unique God-given meaning in a person's life.[6] *Personal vocation* is the great unifying, integrating and animating force in a person's life because Jesus Christ, the Word made flesh, is the beginning and end of all creation. God spoke one Word and this Word holds all meaning.

Just as Christ, the Word, is the only meaning there is for the Father, so "Abba" is the deepest meaning for Jesus. Alphonso believes that the *personal vocation* of Jesus is captured in this one word "Abba". It summed up his whole life and mission. It was at the heart of his controversy with the Scribes and Pharisees. It was his reaction in times of exultant consolation and in the depths of desolation. Jesus' *personal vocation* led him into danger on more than one occasion. In Luke we read how Jesus begins the mission of his "Abba" and the people in the synagogue are so enraged they want to kill him. In the Garden of Gethsemane, Jesus experiences his *personal vocation* as an imminent threat to his life and he grieves and struggles with the will of his "Abba", illustrating, once again, that *personal vocation* is not only a dynamic process but a dangerous one as well.

Concrete History

Our *personal vocation* – our unique divine spark – is the concrete unfolding of our personal story or myth. "It is written into one's concrete history and into the inner dynamism...of one's life."[7]

We grow into our God-given name, without realizing it, until the spiralling touch of God awakens us to the reality of a hidden, deeper Self as a call to further growth. We never fully become our God-given name in this life as the human being is always in a process of becoming. When we are plunged into Christ at baptism, we are uniquely clothed in Christ, but the movement into the depth of Christ lasts a lifetime and is a deepening and dynamic process. The waters of baptism may symbolize the unconscious and our hidden identity which surface to awareness as we journey through life.

In chapter 1, words were described as having a colour, depth and texture and the power to evoke vastly more than they mean. Our *personal vocation* has a shape, a colour a texture which blend with the unfolding fabric of life, thus receiving a new "aspect", a new "colouring", a new "deepening" as life moves on.[8] To take the analogy of fire, the divine spark within each of us shares the same essence as a flame and, while this essence does not change, the spark may fan into a flame and the flame itself may take on new shapes, different colourings and burn more deeply depending on material circumstances. It is important to note also that an individual's *personal vocation* may not sound very unique to other people, but it has the power to evoke profound and unique meaning for that individual person.

Once we have discerned our *personal vocation*, we can look back over our lives and see the unfolding of a unique God-given life-script. Our unique divine spark burns into life, so to speak. This exercise may bring deep consolation for an individual and the awareness that, once named by God, God will never write off an individual. God has branded us on the palm of God's very own hands (cf Is 49:16). The essence of our unique spirit is present throughout life and in essence it does not change. As Alphonso points out, however, this spirit is embodied and the concrete enfleshment of our *personal vocation* will change with changing circumstances. Our life may be described as a trajectory: the curved pathway of our *personal vocation* leading to its fullest manifestation of shape, colour and energy at the resurrection. Gerald O'Mahony S.J. movingly describes the eschaton moment:

God will say one name, and after a hush I will know
he means no-one but me. I do not yet fully know
that name, but I do know the avenue for me marked
your servant has been leading towards it.[9]

For, as Julian of Norwich points out, we are not now as
fully whole in Christ as we will be one day.[10]

Election and Conversion

Alphonso believes that, "The authentic meaning of 'Election' in the process and dynamics of the Ignatian Exercises is
a becoming aware in growing inner freedom of God's
personal design or plan for me."[11] This design is our unrepeatable uniqueness, our deepest and truest Self, our *personal
vocation*. Growth in inner freedom amounts to an inner
spaciousness and a broader vision. It means standing on holy
ground and seeing things "increasingly with God's eyes, no
longer with jaundiced vision".[12] This is metanoia: the taking
hold of the totality of our life and turning it over to God. It
is to plough a new and deeper furrow; to discover the God-
given trajectory in life: the pathway of our *personal vocation*.

Summary

Each one of us is uniquely called and named in Christ Jesus,
the eternal Word made flesh. Since God's eternal Word
holds all meaning, there is a unique expression of the Word
for each one of us. Each one of us has a unique face or
aspect of God in the rich and mutlifaceted personality of
Christ Jesus. This unique aspect is our God-given name,
our deepest identity, our *personal vocation*.

Our *personal vocation* is not on the level of hierarchically
structured vocations. Rather, it is the spirit which gifts with
uniqueness and it is deeper than personae and ego-identity,

and any hierarchical vocation in life. It is the great unifying, integrating and animating force in our life since it is our God-given meaning: a God-given meaning which is continuously reaching new depths. Human beings are always in a process of becoming and so our unique essence blends with the unfolding fabric of life thus receiving a new aspect and a new colouring.

Personal vocation is God's will or personal design for each individual. God's will in its deepest sense is that each person would hear his or her *personal vocation* and embody or incarnate this deep and unique identity. God's will in its deepest sense is that I be the unique individual She-He created me to be.

No better summary could be found than Gerard Manley Hopkins' poem, 'As Kingfishers Catch Fire', in which he beautifully captures the depth of *personal vocation*:

As kingfishers catch fire, dragonflies draw flame:
As tumbled over rim in roundy wells
Stones ring; like each tucked string tells, each hung bell's
Bow swung finds tongue to fling out broad its name;
Each mortal thing does one thing and the same:
Deals out that being indoors each one dwells;
Selves — goes itself; myself it speaks and spells;
Crying W*hat I do is me: for that I came.*

I say more: the just man justices;
Keeps grace: that keeps all his goings graces;
Acts in God's eye what in God's eye he is —
Christ — for Christ plays in ten thousand places,
Lovely in limbs, and lovely in eyes not his
To the Father through the features of men's faces.

NOTES

1 Herbert Alphonso S.J., *The Personal Vocation* (Gujarat, India: Gujarat Sahitya Prakash, 1991) 23.

2 ibid 37.

3 ibid 38.

4 Henri J.M. Nouwen, *Reaching Out* (London: Harper Collins, 1976) 45.

5 Bill Huebsch, *A Spirituality of Wholeness: The New Look at Grace* (Mystic, Connecticut: Twenty-Third Pub., 1988) 28.

6 Herbert Alphonso S.J., op. cit., 34.

7 ibid 51.

8 ibid 54.

9 Gerald O'Mahony S.J., *Finding the Still Point* (Guildford, Surrey: Eagle Pub., 1993) 80. In this little book O'Mahony encourages his readers to listen to their moods and he suggests that one's *personal vocation* or motto is a lodestar which guides individuals to their still point.

10 Brendan Doyle, *Meditations with Julian of Norwich* (Santa Fe, New Mexico: Bear & Co., 1983) 54.

11 Herbert Alphonso S.J., op. cit., 20. At 46/47 Alphonso outlines the growth in inner freedom which takes us from the obvious plane of sin to the level of values and value systems; then to the level of securities guarded in the obscured recesses of the intellect and in the subtle motivations of the will; and finally to the hidden folds of the heart.

12 ibid 47.

Chapter 4

Radical Story-shaping

Personal vocation is written into
one's concrete history...
                    Herbert Alphonso, *The Personal Vocation*

Radical story-shaping is living from our deep spring of inner truth: it is responding to the call to enflesh our God-given name, to incarnate our unique spirit. Radical story-shaping means becoming ever more conscious co-writers with the Word; conscious co-writers of our creation story.

The word "radical" comes from the Latin word *radix* which means root or source. The root of a plant is that hidden and secret part which reaches deep beneath the superficial layer of soil, providing nourishment for the whole plant. Radical story-shaping takes place when we become aware of, and enter into partnership with, that hidden reality deep in the soil of our being; that hidden reality which is our deepest and truest Self rooted in Christ.

However, crossing into the land of this hidden reality – into the land of deep awareness – involves stepping into the area of personal responsibility and choices; and choices beget consequences which are joyful and sorrowful. The call to be our deepest and truest Self is not an invitation to a comfort zone but to a zone of transformation. The story of Moses reminds us that entry into sacred ground is fraught with dangers which play a part in the liberating and transformative process. Abraham's story and Judith's story illustrate that there are dangers, risks and obstacles to be encountered. The story of Jacob reminds us of the woundedness, brokenness and darkness which we will meet on this inner journey to holy ground. The story of Judas alerts us to the existence of pitfalls and zones of entrapment into which we might stumble; it alerts us to the "false kiss" and blindness of betrayal.

Danger, risk and woundedness are aspects of *personal vocation* which Alphonso tends to overlook. For example, Alphonso differentiates between *personal vocation* and hierarchically structured vocations, but he does not indicate how a person might get trapped in hierarchically structured vocation. Frequently, an individual can fail to discriminate between his or her unique God-given identity and the demands made by society. Instead of entering transformative space, one may become trapped in ego or persona ideals because comfort and security are sought rather than truth.

In addition, there is the problem of oppressive structures in society and authority figures who have not discovered the spaciousness of their own *personal vocation*. In *A Wizard of Earthsea*, Ogion warns Ged that danger surrounds power as shadow surrounds light. In theory people are encouraged to be unique but in practice they are pressurized to conform. Our *personal vocation* is our God-given secret in life because that which is deeply and uniquely personal is also ineffable. This secret which we hold and carry, like treasure in earthenware vessels, forms us as unique individuals separate from the collective, but it can also be experienced as a wound which alienates us. Frequently, authority and the collective misunderstand the attempt to live out one's uniqueness and they mete out punishment. Yet our very woundedness and brokenness mothers-forth a desire for relatedness: it is that sacred ground where we meet our God and the rest of broken humanity. Our very woundedness creates space for the Spirit to enter...to sting...to move...to dance...to sing.

Radical story-shaping shakes the earth. It is a sharp sword which ploughs new and deeper furrows. It channels fresh air. It confronts and manoeuvres obstacles in its path. It reaches out. It crosses boundaries. It touches darkness. It connects with light. It opens at the core.

Radical story-shaping is enfleshing our *personal vocation*.

It is embodying our unique God-given spirit. Radical story-shaping means living from the source of our being and there are forces at work in the psyche which can block the pathway to this deep source. In John 14:6 Jesus says: I am the way, and the truth and the life. Following Jesus into transformative space involves a death to persona ideals and ego-control.

Personal vocation has its psychological parallel in Carl Jung's *Personal Myth*. Jung's depth psychology offers an important insight into the journey toward our holy ground and deepest Self. It throws light on dangers and pitfalls and it helps to contextualize the unique spirit of *personal vocation* both in the body and in the outer world. Radical story-shaping is a journey in and through the pages of the world. It is a journey of body-soul-spirit.

Chapter 5

Personal Myth:
The Call to Individuation

Individuation is our waking up to our total selves...
[it] is the "actualizing of the blueprint"...
                              Robert A. Johnson, *Inner Work*

Carl G. Jung's vision of transformative call and the development of personality has important insights for the body-soul-spirit journey. His depth psychology throws light on the experience of call and what might be meant by *personality* and one's deepest and truest *Self*.

Personality

According to Jung, the fullness of human existence is personality and it is everyone's ultimate aim and desire to develop it. Personality means fidelity to the law of one's being which is present from the very beginning as a seed in the child. This seed grows slowly through the different phases of human development, but the fruit of personality is an adult ideal. Personality brings blessing but carries the cost of pain: it is both a charism and a curse.[1]

The human personality consists of consciousness and of an unlimited hinterland of unconscious psyche. Jung has chosen the term *Self* to designate the totality of the person: the whole of conscious and unconscious existence. Becoming a personality means developing our innate germ of wholeness.

Individuation is the term Jung uses to describe this lifelong process of becoming a personality. The goal of individuation

53

is the realization of the Self: our innate pattern of being and our deepest identity. The Self is the most important of the archetypes which Michael Eigen describes as psychic DNA. Archetypes are universal psychological patterns and crystallisations of energy. These patterns and crystallisations uniquely combine in the individual, depending on personal factors, family history and cultural influence.

Jung saw the Self as a God-image or, at least, that it is indistinguishable from one. The use of the term Self, "...serves to express an unknowable essence which we cannot grasp as such, since by definition it transcends our powers of comprehension. It might equally well be called the 'God within us'..."[2] The Self is the ineffable centre of the personality which cannot be fully known or integrated in this life. As we journey through the different stages of life, new aspects of the Self emerge which demand expression. Of these aspects of the Self, Jung found four to be most prominent: the Ego, the Persona, the Shadow and the Anima/Animus.

The Process of Individuation: An Overview

Ego and Self

The Self has a teleological function which means that, from the beginning of infancy, the Self has a purpose and a mission to manifest itself in the individual's life. The first stage of individuation ranges from birth to mid-life, and in this phase the psyche's task is to form a healthy and flexible ego. In Latin the word "ego" means "I". Freud and Jung used "ego" to describe the conscious mind and conscious identity. The formation of a strong ego is vital. The ego is the place where we encounter the Self: it needs to be strong enough to contain the different aspects of the Self and to channel the Self into life and consciousness. Paradoxically, this strong ego-state recognises and accepts its own limitations. Dialogue between the ego and the Self involves the adoption of an attentive, listening stance towards the Centre of the whole personality and the humility to acknowledge a reality far greater than itself.

Persona

Related to ego-consciousness is the development of persona. The word "persona" comes from the Latin and it refers to the mask worn by ancient actors. Jung uses it to describe the mask or role which one presents to the outer world as a means of social adaptation, but it is not identical with individuality. The persona is a necessary social "face" for walking the stage of life and it may change in different situations and circumstances. However, there is a danger that our persona or personae might set and become fixtures, thus preventing the awareness and recognition of our inner "face": of our unique and deepest identity. If a person identifies with his or her persona, then it becomes detrimental to the growth and development of personality.

Identification with the persona leads to rigid and stereotypical behaviour and the formation of a pseudo-ego which is fragile and brittle. People who identify with persona play their role in inappropriate places. For example, it is the doctor who always insists on her title; the army commander who raises his children with the discipline of a military camp; the priest who can never appear without his or her collar. Such identification with the persona forms a fragile ego because a sense of identity is based on function or *doing* rather than on *being*.

The differentiation between ego and persona is necessary for the development of personal moral responsibility. As Edward C. Whitmont points out, a role-identified non-personality will hide behind collective morality instead of developing personal, ethical principles. In other words, "Crossing over into the land of awareness necessarily means crossing into the land of responsibility."[3]

The healthy development of ego and persona is a necessary prerequisite for entering the second phase of the individuation process which is the main focus of Jung's analytical psychology. The process of individuation proceeds because of the encounter between the conscious and the unconscious in liminal space and transitional territory. It involves the movement from the ego to the Self as the centre of the psyche. It is a painful process made difficult by the pervasive concern for security but it also brings joy.

The Shadow

The encounter between the persona and the shadow is an important first step in crossing over into the land of awareness and responsibility. Heinz Westman points out that the persona is not restricted to our dealings with the outer world. We can turn the persona toward the inner world also. In an effort to "save face", we can "set our face against" the shadow side of the personality. If a person continues to repress and suppress this shadow side it will be detrimental to the development of personality. The integration of the shadow into ego-consciousness is a necessary and painful task on the journey toward the Self. In a powerful moment in *A Wizard of Earthsea*, Ged faces his own shadow across the desert of the sea:

> In silence, man and shadow met face to face, and stopped. Aloud and clearly, breaking that old silence, Ged spoke the shadow's name, and in the same moment the shadow spoke without lips or tongue, saying the same word: Ged. And the two voices were one voice.
>
> Ged reached out his hands, dropping his staff, and took hold of his shadow, of the black self that reached out to him. Light and darkness met, and joined, and were one.[4]

In that moment Ged experienced wholeness and healing:

> "Estarriol", he said, "look, it is done. It is over." He laughed. "The wound is healed," he said, "I am

whole, I am free." Then he bent over and hid his face
in his arms, weeping like a boy [5]

A relational axis exists between the persona and the
shadow, through which the shadow can manifest itself in
persona-based behaviours, reactions, one-sidedness and
rigidities. These are encountered in projective ways and
blamed on other people. Since the shadow is an unconscious part of the personality, we encounter it in projections
and in dreams. John A. Sanford points out that a study of
humour, slips of the tongue, unconscious forgetting, and
our fantasies can also hint at the nature of our shadow.

Projections are very important in getting to know our
shadow. However, if they are not recognized as such they
can obscure the individuality of other people and destroy
genuine relationship.

Jung notes that no one becomes conscious of the shadow
side of personality without considerable moral effort. In his
book, *Evil: The Shadow Side of Reality*, John A. Sanford
discusses the positive and negative aspects of the shadow.
He notes that if we project our own hated dark side onto
other people, we will see them and relate to them according
to this despised projection. Shadow projections are the root
cause of racial prejudice, sectarianism and religious intolerance. The ethical implications which arise from the
persona-shadow axis are quite clear and much examination
of consciousness is needed to disentangle what is really at
issue in our relationships. Perhaps spiritual discernment
takes place at the point where the unconscious – through
the voices of the Persona, Shadow, Anima/Animus – tries
to break through deafness and conscious efforts to ignore
truth. It is a difficult and painful task as the shadow conflicts
with persona ideals. However, the pain cannot be avoided if
we are to journey towards the Centre and discover our
personal myth and meaning in life. Jung discovered that the
shadow is 90% gold, and that it consists of good qualities as
well as reprehensible tendencies. Marie-Louise von Franz

explains that whether the shadow acts as enemy or friend depends on the individual. It becomes hostile only when it is disregarded, unappreciated, or misunderstood. We must befriend our shadow if we want to develop personality and discover our uniqueness. "The shadow", Edward C. Whitmont states, "is the door to our individuality... There is in fact no access to the unconscious and to our own reality but through the shadow."[6]

Anima and Animus

The shadow has been compared, by Whitmont, to an unknown inland lake, and the anima and animus to the ocean. It is more difficult to gain insight into the anima and animus, and, as Whitmont points out, "They connect us to the limitlessness of the psyche itself."[7] Jung describes the anima and animus as the foundation stones of the psychic structure. As archetypes their contents can be integrated and their effects made conscious, but they in themselves remain autonomous and beyond conscious integration.

Jung saw the anima and animus as a contrasexual dynamic, with the anima personifying feminine psychological tendencies in a man and the animus personifying masculine psychological tendencies in a woman. He describes the anima and animus as mediators between the conscious and unconscious and as personifications of the latter. However, in the light of clinical experience and of feminist criticism, the concept of the anima and animus as a contrasexual dynamic *only* is being revised. Each person, regardless of gender, contains unassimilated active (animus) and receptive (anima) energies.

Jung saw the anima and the animus as the psychological parallel to the "soul" in religious language. The anima is the feminine soul image in a man and the animus, according to Jung, is the masculine soul image in a woman. However, Emma Jung, Carl's wife, and other "Jungian" women have challenged the identification of animus with soul, and they argue that a woman's soul is also feminine, and that the animus is the spirit in woman which guides her to her soul.

Through integration, the anima becomes eros and it gives relationship and relatedness to a man's consciousness. The animus, through integration, becomes a logos and gives to woman's consciousness a capacity for reflection, deliberation and self-knowledge. Jung uses the symbolism of Eve, Helen of Troy, the Virgin Mary and Sophia to describe the development of the anima in men. The goal of the Eve stage is biological fertility, that of Helen the physical and biological union of the opposites. The goal of the Mary stage is spiritual fertility and that of Sophia/Sapientia the psychological union of the opposites. William Johnston S.J. interprets Jung's symbolism as saying there is a growth toward mysticism which is a very human process. Marie-Louise von Franz outlines the fourfold development of the animus in women. He initially appears as mere physical power; then as the possessor of initiative and of the capacity for planned action. Thirdly, he manifests as the word or logos and, finally, as the mediator of the religious experience whereby life requires new meaning.[8]

Since human development does not take place in a vacuum, the anima in a man is influenced by the mother, and the animus in a woman is shaped by the father. Like the shadow, the anima and animus can manifest negative aspects. For example, the negative aspect of a man's anima can manifest itself in irritability and moodiness. The negative aspect of a woman's animus can manifest itself in argumentativeness and stubbornness. However, they are also invaluable companions: they hold the key to the world of the archetypes where we discover our personal meaning and myth in life.

The Psychological Significance of Vocation

The experience of being called is an essential feature of individuation. According to Jung, vocation is that irrational factor which fatefully persuades a person to climb out of unconscious identity with the collective and to walk a unique path in life. He states:

> True personality always has vocation and believes in it, has fidelity to it as to God...this vocation acts like a law of God from which there is no escape...Who has vocation hears the voice of the inner man; he is called.[9]

Jungian therapist, Marie-Louise von Franz, points out that the call to individuation is frequently experienced as a wounding of the personality. The ego's awareness of the Self and of its imperatives is accompanied by suffering and initial shock. This experience of suffering and shock has the significance of a "call".[10] The ego now realises that it is relative to a greater Centre. Sacrifice of the ego goes hand in hand with this relativisation, and the individual may experience intense fear and anxiety. Since the relativisation of the ego and the manifestation of the Self is an ongoing dynamic and lifelong process, "Individuation is in itself a kind of wound," as John A. Sanford states, "and there is a connection between becoming whole and experiencing one's illness and woundedness. We can even speak of individuation as a 'divine wound'."[11] Sanford highlights the story of Jacob as the classic case of a divine wound. This wound allows the life and energy of the unconscious, and of one's hidden identity, to flow into consciousness.

Refusal to heed the call to individuation is fraught with danger. If the ego does not co-operate with the activated Self it will experience disturbing symptoms such as neurosis, psychosomatic illness and distressing dream-imagery.

The ultimate consequence of not answering the call is that one remains nameless, cut off from genuine individuality. As Jung notes, the inner voice is the voice of a fuller life. Turning a deaf ear to this voice results in self-dispossession of an ever-broadening consciousness of the inner land, and of the wellspring of inner truth. It means being confined to a zone of entrapment. This zone of entrapment has serious consequences both for the individual and for society, and it will be discussed in greater detail in a section on the persona-shadow axis.

Even though the inner voice is the voice of a fuller life, it is important to point out that, "The problems of the inner voice are full of hidden pits and snares. It is a most dangerous and slippery region."[12] Individuation is a *dynamic process* and there are tendencies in the psyche that can lead us off the pathway to our true Self, off the pathway to the divine fire at the Centre. Robert M. Doran points out the danger of identifying with collective consciousness and the danger of surrendering to or being inflated by the collective unconscious. "In either case," he states, "one is not assuming responsibilty for self- and world-constitution, is not fulfilling one's unique vocation within the universe."[13]

The Example of Jesus

Jung holds up the life of Jesus as a shining example of individuation: one who heard the call and embraced the destiny implicit in it. He lived his own truth and was absolutely and unconditionally faithful to the law of his inner being, to the voice of his "Abba". As Jung points out, the life of Jesus has been the sacred symbol in Western civilisation for two thousand years and is the prototype of the only meaningful life. Jung proclaimed Jesus as the still living myth of our culture and as our culture hero. Through the example of his life, Jesus illustrates the archetype of the Self.[14]

As a psychologist Jung had no alternative but to state that Christ is a symbol of the Self. From his scientific perspective, Jung saw Christianity as a religion founded upon the self-realisation of Jesus. Our story, he emphasizes, is not meant to be mere imitation but the story of a life lived as truly as Christ lived his. Real *imitatio Christi* is walking the path of individuation.

The theologian, on the other hand, would state that the Self is a symbol of Christ. For the believer these two views need not be exclusive. As the incarnate Word, Jesus Christ is the symbol par excellence. He is a symbol of the Self and, as little words contained in this eternal Word, each individual's Self is a symbol of Christ. In other words, real *imitatio Christi* is enfleshing our God-given uniqueness as creatures created through the power of the eternal Word.

Personal Meaning and Personal Myth

Carl Jung describes neurosis as an attempt to escape from one's inner voice and from vocation. If we are unfaithful to the law of our being and do not develop personality, then we fail to realize the meaning of our life. "A psychoneurosis", Jung states, "must be understood as the suffering of a human being who has not discovered what life means for him."[15] In his clinical experience, Jung observed that the fundamental problem of each patient, in the second half of life, was the loss of religious outlook. He maintained that the gain of religious outlook was necessary for real healing. Jung, approaching religion as a psychologist, points out that religious outlook has nothing to do with a particular creed or church membership. Creeds are dogmatized prescriptions of original religious experience. As stated earlier, the literal meaning of the word "religion" is to "bind" to something, and this is the sense in which Jung uses it. We are bound, in Jung's view, to the numinous encounter of the Self as Other: the soul is religious by nature, and religions arise from the natural life of the unconscious psyche.

Jung describes dogma as a distillation of "sacred history" and of the myth of the divine being. He maintains that all dogma can be traced back to original psychic experience. Regarding the Christian religion, he believes that the bridge from dogma to the inner experience of the individual has broken down. There needs to be a new assimilation of the traditional myth which Jung sees as the idea that everyone is Christ. The experience and expression of our own inner divine spark, or fire, provide a sense of being held in a meaningful existence; and, as mature personalities, we are able to hold our own God.

Myths are fundamental expressions of human nature and its experiences. They carry the meaning of human existence in the cosmos. Jolande Jacobi explains mythology as the form of manifestation adopted by the archetypes in the process of becoming symbols. "There is a primordial kinship", she states, "between the great traditional mythologies with their mythologems and the archetypes with their symbols, which have condensed into 'individual mythologies' in the individual psyche."[16] In other words, collective and individual symbols arise from the same forming capacity in the psyche. This means that an individual symbol... enables the individual psyche to preserve its unique form of expression and at the same time to merge it with the universally human, collective symbol.[17] The spontaneous unfolding of symbol in the individual psyche gives rise to our personal myth which is intertwined with universal myth.

Jung stresses that we do not invent myth. Myth is the revelation of divine life in humankind and it speaks to us as a word of God.

Jesus Christ, the incarnate Word, makes tangible the myth of the divine Primordial Man. He is the archetypal Self, the invisible Centre of energy which manifests as a collective symbol and desires to incarnate in the individual ego in a uniquely personal way. In other words, there is a facet of the multifaceted collective symbol which is proper to each individual.

The uniquely personal manifestation of symbol in the individual psyche mediates personal meaning and demands to be written into our concrete history. It is a never-ending myth as the person is always in a process of becoming. As

Jolande Jacobi explains, "The meaning of a symbol can appear in an ever-changing light or open up to us gradually, so that this meaning and even the very form of the symbol are placed in continuously new contexts and transformed accordingly."[18] The symbol has roots in the core of our being, in the secret depths of the soul where there is an abundance of life. The symbol is a *psychic transformer* of energy which deepens the pathway to the divine fire at the centre by dissolving and transforming obstructions.

The Transcendent Function

The conscious and unconscious aspects of symbol give it a capacity for reconciling pairs of opposites which Jung calls the *transcendent function*. Sometimes the process of individuation can come to a standstill, with the individual sensing a loss of meaning and alienation from personal myth. The *transcendent function* enables the process of individuation to proceed, since the reconciling symbol facilitates transition, giving new directive in times of inner tension and conflict. The transcendent function enables us to hold the tension of life with a certain lightness. The words "despise"... "inferior"... "weakness"... "limitations"... hold the key to the *transcendent function*. The genuine treasure is hidden in the areas which we despise most. The potential for transformation is in our weakness and the new holistic attitude which arises with the *transcendent function* is the psychological parallel to the birth of Christ in a lowly stable. The reconciling symbol expresses the law of our being and leads to the revelation of our individual and unique essence. The new directive which accompanies the transcendent function leads to a further unfolding of our *personal myth* and meaning in life.

Summary

The call to individuation is the call to embrace our innermost and incomparable uniqueness. It is a call to ego-consciousness to relate to the greater reality of the Self: the centre of the total personality. Jung postulates that the Self is an *imago Dei* and that myth speaks to us as a word of God. The unfolding of symbols in the individual psyche gives rise to our *personal myth* and meaning in life. It is a deep and demanding process which involves danger, risk and challenge. It brings about an encounter with woundedness and pain, but awareness also brings joy and greater freedom. Jung signposts the way to the inner marriage – to the deepening relationship between the ego and the Self – and he warns about slippery regions. These slippery regions have hidden pits and negative aspects, and they have snares and zones of entrapment which might lead us off the pathway to the divine wedding and the divine fire at the Centre.

NOTES

1 Cf Carl G. Jung, *The Integration of the Personality* (London: Routledge & Kegan Paul, (1940) 1963). The life of Jesus illustrates that personality is both a charism and a curse. He had to hold the charism of his vocation and the curse of his life and death on a tree in creative tension (cf Dt 21:23; Gal 3:13,14).
2 Carl G. Jung, *Two Essays on Analytical Psychology, CW VII* (London: Routledge & Kegan Paul, 1953) par. 399.
3 Heinz Westman, *The Springs of Creativity: The Bible and the Creative Process of the Psyche* (Wilmette, Illinois: Chiron Pub., 1986) 161.
4 Ursula Le Guin, op. cit., 197/198.
5 ibid 199.
6 Whitmont, Edward C.; THE SYMBOLIC QUEST: BASIC CONCEPTS OF ANALYTICAL PSYCHOLOGY Copyright © 1969 by C.G. Jung Foundation, 1978 Princeton University Press. 164/165.
Reprinted by permission of Princeton University Press
7 ibid 215.
8 Cf Marie-Louise Von Franz, "The Process of Individuation" in C.G. Jung, ed., *Man and His Symbols* (London: Picador/Pan, 1978) 206/207.
9 Carl G. Jung, *The Integration of the Personality*, 291/292. At 293 Jung points out that the clearest example of vocation, or being addressed by a voice, is found in the confessions of the Old Testament prophets.

10   Cf Marie-Louise Von Franz, The Process of Individuation in C.G. Jung, ed., *Man and His Symbols*, 181.

11   John A. Sanford, *Healing and Wholeness*, Copyright © 1977 Paulist Press, New York, 33.

12   Carl G. Jung, *The Integration of the Personality*, 304.

13   Robert M. Doran S.J., Jungian Psychology and Christian Spirituality in Robert L. Moore, ed., *Carl Jung and Christian Spirituality*, Copyright © 1988 Paulist Press, New York/Mahwah 84–96 at 87.

14   Cf Carl G. Jung, *The Integration of the Personality*, 297/298. As pointed out in chapter 3, Herbert Alphonso S.J. believes that Jesus' inner voice or *personal vocation* may be summed up in the word "Abba". Cf Carl G. Jung, *Aion: Researches into the Phenomenology of the Self, CW IX, II* (London: Routledge & Kegan Paul, (1959) 1968) at pars. 122/123 where Jung poses the question, Is the Self a symbol of Christ, or is Christ a symbol of the Self?

15   Carl G. Jung, *Modern Man in Search of a Soul* (London: Routledge & Kegan Paul, (1933) 1961) 260. Jung notes that all creativeness in the realm of the spirit, and every psychic advance arise from a state of mental suffering.

16   Jacobi, Jolande; COMPLEX, ARCHETYPE, SYMBOL IN THE PSYCHOLOGY OF C. G. JUNG. Copyright © 1959 by Bollinger Foundation Inc. New York, NY. 109.

Reprinted by permission of Princeton University Press

17   ibid 104.

18   ibid 116.

Chapter 6

Inner Marriage: Symbol of Wholeness and Holiness

*For that our soul cleave with all its power
is the one desire of our Lover.*
> B. Doyle, *Meditations with Julian of Norwich*

Personal vocation is an interpersonal love relationship holding the secret of unity and integration at the heart of life.[1] Individuation and the unfolding of *personal myth* is a process of integration often described as a mystical marriage. In this chapter we will look at the inner marriage as a symbol of wholeness and holiness: as a symbol of union with self, others and God.

Invitation to a Divine Wedding

The call to individuation is an invitation to a wedding. Jung describes the individuation process as a *mysterium coniunctionis* in which the Self is experienced as a nuptial union of opposite halves. It is a divine wedding because of the numinous aspect of the Self.

Very often, the messenger of this wedding invitation is Neurotic Suffering and our brokenness and woundedness is the privileged place where the call to transformation is heard. This is the painful yet privileged place where we cry out for personal meaning and integration, for connectedness and relatedness. The word "wholeness" conveys a sense of several aspects or parts working together as a unity. If the unconscious aspect of the psyche is ignored it will make its presence felt through secondary process, such as neurotic suffering, psychosomatic symptoms and body language. When a person recognizes the unconscious as a partner, and enters the process of individuation, then neurotic suffering may be transformed into redemptive suffering. One meaning of the verb "to redeem" is "to reclaim". The process of individuation is a gradual reclaiming of the unlimited hinterland of unconscious psyche.

In Christian spirituality we owe the terminology of spiritual marriage to St Teresa of Avila and St John of the Cross, but the idea of spiritual weddings and divine nuptials existed much earlier. As already pointed out, the symbolic language of betrothal and marriage does not surface in Ignatian spirituality. Instead of "marriage" Alphonso uses the description "interpersonal love relationship" and there are sexual undertones in the idea of "putting on Christ".

In the New Testament, the call to integration and transformation takes place in the region of Caesarea Philippi. This is where Jesus poses the question: Who do you say that I am? This is where he foretells his own suffering, death and resurrection. This is where he spells out the price of discipleship (cf Mk 8:27-37; Mt 16:13-28). Caesarea Philippi may be taken as a metaphor for that privileged place where we are confronted with our human weakness and limitation (cf Mk 8:32,33), that place where we hear the voice of the divine Other asking us for recognition and asking us to transcend ego-identity. However, once entered upon, abandonment of the Way is perilous. This is evident in the fate of Judas, who, according to The Acts of the Apostles, invested in a field which was a zone of death: "...falling headlong, he burst open in the middle and all his bowels gushed out" (Acts 1:18). There was little integration between Judas' head and his gut; no deep inner marriage of the masculine logos and feminine eros.

Healing, Wholeness and Holiness

Desire for the healing of neurotic suffering may be the first step on the journey towards realizing our *personal myth* and discovering our God-given meaning in life. Both the process of individuation and the journey of discipleship transform this suffering into redemptive suffering. It is a reclaiming of sacred space where one has a sense of belonging, of love and of meaning. It is that sacred space where the Self and ego can say: "We are married"; where God and the individual can proclaim: "We are one." It is that sacred space where:

> The wolf shall live with the lamb,
>> the leopard shall lie down with the kid,
>> the calf and the lion and the fatling together,
>> and a little child shall lead them.
> The cow and the bear shall graze,
>> their young shall lie down together;
>> and the lion shall eat straw like the ox.
> The nursing child shall play over
>> the hole of the asp,
>> and the weaned child shall put
>> its hand on the adder's den.
> They will not hurt or destroy
>> on all my holy mountain;
>> for the earth will be full of the
>> knowledge of the Lord
>> as the waters cover the sea (Is 11:6-9).

This passage from Isaiah may symbolize conflictual parts of our personality which are reconciled on God's holy mountain. We all have a wolf-side and a lamb-side; we hold an innocent child and an astute adult; there is an inner hero/heroine and an inner coward; an inner saint and a sinner. Robert A. Johnson stresses the importance of belief in one Source from which the diversity of life flows and to which this life returns. "We could not find the courage to face up to the terrible divisions in us," he states, "unless we felt instinctively that the conflicts must eventually resolve, the warring parts come together in peace, the fragmentation finally reveal a deeper reality, an underlying fundamental unity and meaning in life."[2]

A Maturing Partnership

The process of individuation, the process of becoming whole, demands a maturing partnership between the ego and the unconscious. Metaphorically speaking, this maturing partnership involves the building of a bridge between the island (ego) and the large hinterland (unconscious). This bridge is built with the natural fabric of dream-symbols and active imagination.

In the beginning, the island (ego) is one with the large hinterland (unconscious) and the first stage of individuation leads to its differentiation. In this phase a baby grows and develops, gradually becoming aware of his or her own identity as distinct from others. There are four stages in this first phase of individuation. In the first stage there is no distinction between the world, the body, the soul and the spirit: there is the original state of oneness. So, the first step is separation from the world. This results in the original state of oneness being split into two entities. The body, soul and spirit remain one entity, but this entity is now separate from the world. The second step is separation from the body which leads to the third stage of three entities: world; body; soul-spirit. The third step is separation from the spirit which results in the fourth stage of four entities. These four entities of world; body; soul; spirit are now differentiated in the individual but not in complete consciousness. The process of differentiation continues in the second phase of individuation.

The second phase of individuation belongs to adulthood

and involves the movement of the ego and the unconscious back toward each other and their conscious marriage. Edward F. Edinger represents the movements of the two phases of individuation in diagrammatic form. The movement in the first phase is a threefold separation and that in the second phase a threefold *coniunctio*, since, as Jung points out, only separated things can unite. The fruit of this marriage is the development of a unique personality:

Phase 1		Phase 2
1 [world – body – soul – spirit] *step a: separation from world*	O	1 [unus mundus (one world)] *3rd coniunctio*
2 [world] [body – soul – spirit] *step b: separation from mother*	O O	2 [world] [body – soul – spirit] *2nd coniunctio*
3 [world] [body] [soul – spirit] *step c: separation from father*	O O O	3 [world] [body] [soul – spirit] *1st coniunctio*
4 [world] [body] [soul] [spirit]	O O O O	4 [world] [body] [soul] [spirit][3]

It is important to point out that while the main focus of the first phase is differentiation, both differentiation and union occur in the second phase. In the first conjunction soul and spirit unite to form a fuller separation from the body and the world. This is the first step in a conscious marriage or synthesis. The individual needs to differentiate the various sub-personalities or archetypal figures in the psyche before they can be integrated.

As is evident from Edinger's diagram, the journey into the realm of spirit is also a journey of the body and of the soul lived out in the world. The first conjunction of soul and spirit is an intellectual harmony which only makes sense if it is experienced in the body and is incarnated. Much of our physical illness betrays a dichotomy between the mind and the body. The process of individuation takes us into the depths of incarnation and into the depths of creation. It heightens our awareness of interdependence and of being part of the whole, of being part of nature and of the whole universe. The second phase of the individuation process will now be dealt with in more detail.

The First Conjunction:
Unio mentalis/Self-knowledge

Nigredo

The first stage of the *coniunctio* is called *unio mentalis* where the soul and spirit unite in a mental union and separate from the body. This mental union, and separation from the body, frees the rational mind from disturbing bodily appetites, instincts and desires. It involves a death process of the dark matter which is the body, and a sublimation of soul-spirit. The ego is separate from the half-animal state of unconsciousness and is strong enough to take a critical and objective stance toward the demands of the body. This first union, as Jung points out, creates the mental discipline of wisdom, but the head is cut off from the body and is not a desirable state for the long-term.

In psychological and alchemical language, this stage means knowledge of oneself. Jung describes self-knowledge as an adventure that carries us far and deep. It is a knowledge reaching beyond knowledge of the ego, and it carries us into the *nigredo* or darkness which produces suffering.

This suffering largely results from the interplay between the persona and the shadow. As already stated, the persona is a necessary social "face" for walking the stage of life and it helps us to deal with and relate to the collective. The shadow, on the other hand, is the door to our individuality. Edward C. Whitmont points out that, "Collectivity and individuality are a pair of polar opposites; hence there is an oppositional and compensatory relationship between persona and shadow."[4] For example, the brighter the persona, the darker the shadow. Paradoxically, to achieve individual wholeness, to secure the integrity of the inner land, we must risk our virtue like Judith in the Old Testament: the bright persona must befriend its dark shadow.

Befriending our shadow means, in part, accepting ourselves and loving ourselves as sinners. We cannot truly love God without accepting and loving the whole of ourselves; we cannot stand in empathy with our neighbour until compassion for self has been experienced. Jung notes that we are encouraged, in the name of Christ, to love the beggar, to love our enemies, to forgive all those who hurt us, and that these are great virtues. Then he poses the question:

> But what if I should discover that the least among them all, the poorest of all beggars, the most impudent of all offenders, yea the very fiend himself – that these are within me, and that I myself stand in need of the alms of my own kindness, that I myself am the enemy who must be loved – what then? [5]

Then we condemn and rage against this villain or poor beggar within, and we forget the commandment, You must love your neighbour as yourself:

> We deny ever having met this least among the lowly in ourselves, and had it been God himself who drew near to us in this despicable form, we should have denied him a thousand times before a single cock had crowed.[6]

If we pray like the Pharisee, thanking God that we are not like other people, such as thieves, rogues, adulterers and tax collectors, then we will never discover the true God (cf Lk 18:9-14). It is only when we dialogue with and befriend our shadow that we can confront the other pairs of psychic opposites, thus discovering our God-given individuality and entering into right relationship with God and others.

The shadow is the dark passageway to the bridal chamber.

It is a journey of dark incomprehensibility: the confusion we face in the mystery of being loved sinners. Gerard Manley Hopkins has captured the mystery of being a broken sinner, yet precious and loved, in his paradoxical image of a poor potsherd and an immortal diamond.

Hopkin's own struggle with darkness is evident in poems such as 'Carrion Comfort' which ends with the line:

> Of now done darkness I wretch lay wrestling with
> (my God!) my God.

In the poem, 'I Wake and Feel the Fell of Dark', Hopkins experiences the bitter taste of himself:

> ...I am gall, I am heartburn. God's most deep decree
> Bitter would have me taste, my taste was me...

If we are to come home to ourselves and to the light, we, like Jacob in the Old Testament and like Hopkins, must wrestle with the word of God which reveals areas of darkness. To savour the sweetness of ourselves, we must also taste the bitterness.

The journey to inner marriage and wholeness involves struggle and conflict; it involves walking into the darkness and holding disturbing soul experiences. There is no other road to spiritual enlightenment, and, therefore, it is unwise to embark on the journey without the necessary food of love, of hope in the light, and of belief in an underlying unity and meaning in life. If we go unprepared for the darkness and fall into a sleep of unawareness, we will not see the brightness of the wedding hall nor taste the flavour of the wedding banquet (cf Mt 25:1-13).

Albedo

In the first stage of the *coniunctio*, the symbolism of the *albedo*, or whitening process, also enters and this whitening process may be compared to the purgative way in the classical three ways of Christianity. These three ways are the Purgative Way, the Illuminative Way and the Unitive Way and each way will be introduced in the relevant stage of individuation.

The task of the purgative way is self-knowledge and it is often called the night of the senses. The night of the senses corresponds to the first *coniunctio* in which the soul and spirit are united but are separate from the body. Both processes may be described as a mortification of the body and a sublimation of soul-spirit.

In the Ignatian tradition, the First Week of the *Spiritual Exercises* corresponds to the purgative way (cf Ex no 10). This First Week is a search for true self-knowledge which brings us face to face with the pattern of our own sinfulness and our own shadow in the personal unconscious (cf Ex no 56-60). The more archetypal and collective shadow emerges in the cosmic sin of the angels and of Adam and Eve (cf Ex no 51/52).

In the first conjunction, and in its corresponding purgative way, it is necessary to face cosmic and personal darkness. However, it is important not to overfocus on the darkness, but to keep the whitening and purifying process of love in view. We must befriend our shadow: we must allow the whole of ourselves to be loved.

The Second Conjunction: Body-Soul-Spirit

Rubedo

In the second stage of the *coniunctio* the spirit-soul partnership, or *unio mentalis*, is reunited with the body. The body is now accepted and loved in the light of paradoxical wholeness. As Jung states, "The reuniting of the spiritual position with the body obviously means that insights gained should be made real."[7] In other words, the second stage demands that self-knowledge and insight be incarnated. The spirit-soul-body union takes the mental discipline of wisdom a step further and manifests the wise man and woman. Abstract wisdom is now incarnated. Wisdom is no longer a mere mental theory but radiates through flesh and bone, and is a full-blooded reality. It calls for the concrete living out of our paradoxical wholeness.

This is the *rubedo* stage in the transformative process which brings the "redness" of life. John A. Sanford notes that becoming whole necessitates being involved with life. "Our life", he states, "must have a story to it if we are to become whole, and this means we must come up against something; otherwise a story can't take place."[8] Our personal myth is not lived in isolation from other people's stories. Likewise, our *personal vocation* is written into our concrete history and into unfolding encounters with other people and events. The call to individuation, the call to be our deepest and truest Self, is an invitation to outer relatedness as well as inner relatedness.

The reuniting of the *unio mentalis* with the body has two parts in the alchemical recipe: a) the extraction of the *caelum* and b) the mixing process.

The *caelum* is the heavenly substance, or deepest truth, or *imago Dei*, which is hidden in the human body and needs to be drawn out and discovered. The *caelum* is then mixed with the following ingredients:

- the honey of desire and pleasure which also carries the danger of sticky, deadly, worldly attachments;
- the flower of wholeness, healing and meaning (Chelidonia);
- the plant of memory and recollection (Rosemary);
- the plant of sexual libido or energy which unites the opposites (Mercurialis);
- the flower of blood and passion (Red Lily).

Jung points out that this second stage of union is particularly important for the attainment of the complete conjunction i.e. union with the *unus mundus*.

This second stage in the transformative process may be compared to the illuminative way in the spiritual tradition. The self-knowledge and the spiritual insights which surface in the illuminative way impact significantly on daily living. Jaundiced vision is gradually yielding to a new way of looking at and understanding reality. Good and bad, saint and sinner can be seen and accepted in the light of God's love.

The Second Week of the *Ignatian Exercises* is comparable to the *rubedo* stage and to the illuminative way. In this Week the retreatant is challenged to put his or her insights at the service of Christ and of others (cf Ex no 10).

Third Conjunction: Union with the World

The man or woman who has been reconnected with the body has a sense of being grounded, and longs for the third union which is the *unus mundus*, or union with the world. The individual desires the original state of oneness with the whole cosmos. In this stage the ego is united with the Self and with the world. These are the split seconds when we feel, like Ged in *A Wizard of Earthsea*, that we are words spoken by the sunlight, and that we are really one with all of creation and understand its language and shapes.

The shadow, which we cast in this light, is the dark passageway to the bridal chamber where the masculine and feminine energies unite to give birth to the Self. This marriage represents the archetype of wholeness which, in Jungian thought, is the integration of the conscious and unconscious poles of the personality. Here there is a conscious awareness of the state of oneness.

Paradoxically, the Self is that energetic force which initiates and prompts the marriage of ego-consciousness with the unconscious, and, at the same time, is the child born of the marriage. Spiritually speaking, God is the initiating power which gives birth to God in the life of the individual.

In alchemy the union of the masculine and the feminine, of the spiritual and the material gave rise to an eternal body which the alchemists called a *lapis Philosophorum* or Philosophers' stone. In the words of T.S. Eliot:

> Here the impossible union
>> Of spheres of existence is actual,
> Here the past and future
>> Are conquered and reconciled.
>
> *(The Dry Salvages, Four Quartets)*[9]

With the creation of the Philosophers' stone, time and eternity are synchronized. This *coniunctio* represents a liminal, transitional state: an altered state of consciousness which reaches its full potential only in the resurrected eternal body since ego-consciousness is too narrow to fully contain it. Jung points out that the alchemists never reached the point of producing the *lapis* with its miraculous powers and, similarly, psychic wholeness is always a step beyond our experience since there is always something new to be integrated.

This third stage of the *coniunctio* corresponds to the unitive way in the spiritual tradition. The unitive way describes our experience of union with God, having first faced self-knowledge, darkness and daily living. This inner and outer facing is done in the growing light of faith, hope and love. The individual comes to view reality more and more through the eyes of God. He or she experiences being knit to God (cf Ps 139), yet the transcendent God is always beyond grasp or understanding.

The Philosophers' stone has its parallel in the resurrected, eternal Christ who becomes the cornerstone rejected by the builders. In the Fourth Week of the *Ignatian Exercises*, the individual participates in the life of the risen Christ and is united with him. However, Christ in his entire reality cannot be held either (cf Jn 20:17). Union with him is an ever deepening process: it is a maturing partnership which brings us ever closer to our true Self, to others and to the Godhead.

Society and the Three-fold *Coniunctio*

A cursory glance at our society reveals the need for these three stages of union. In some areas of society the pleasure principle and instant gratification abound, with little discipline when it comes to bodily urges and bodily demands. In many instances folly rules the waves and wise thinking is sorely lacking.

In other areas wise thinking and theory abound but, largely, it remains in head centres and its effects haven't reached gut level. Many people are enlightened at a mental level but suffer stress, tension and illness at a physical level. We read and hear very wise insights and very wise words, but how much flesh and bone actually radiates wisdom and wholeness? There is a great need in Western Christian spirituality to reconnect with the body, and to live out our humanity to the full by following the way of the Incarnation.

The growing need for intimacy with the world and universe is evident in this ecological and cosmological age. We need to listen with the heart to earth and sky. Our inner *caelum*, or divine spark, needs to merge with the ever ancient and ever new flame at the heart of the whole cosmos. We need to realize that we do, indeed, walk on holy ground, and that we share a sacred habitat with creatures wild and tame, and with vegetation of every shape and hue. Like Ged in *A Wizard of Earthsea*, we need to know a plant in all its seasons and learn its true name which is much more than its immediate use. We need to heed the warning of the Master Hand who counselled Ged as follows:

> But you must not change one thing, one pebble, one grain of sand, until you know what good and evil will follow on the act. The world is in balance, in Equilibrium.[10]

As God calls every human being by name, we, too, are called to name our environment and its creatures with personal names and build an intimate, caring relationship. Then we will understand the song of the universe and be one with its mystical movement.

Summary

Both *individuation* and *personal vocation* are a process of integration leading to wholeness and unity. This process of integration involves a maturing partnership between ego-consciousness and our hidden identity in the unconscious; a maturing partnership between body, soul and spirit lived out in the world. This maturing partnership, or inner marriage, involves a descent into darkness – a purifying darkness – and a journey through the redness of life towards the white stone at the Centre. It is a journey toward wholeness and holiness; a journey back toward the original state of oneness. It is a quest of Love.

NOTES

1 Cf Herbert Alphonso S.J., op. cit., 27.
2 Robert A. Johnson, *Inner Work* (New York: HarperSanFrancisco/HarperCollins, (1986) 1989) 37.
3 Edward F. Edinger, *The Mysterium Lectures: A Journey through C. G. Jung's Mysterium Coniunctionis* (Toronto: Inner City Books, 1995) 282.
4 Whitmont, Edward C.; THE SYMBOLIC QUEST: BASIC CONCEPTS OF ANALYTICAL PSYCHOLOGY. Copyright © 1969 by C.G. Jung Foundation, 1978 Princeton University Press. 159.
     Reprinted by permission of Princeton University Press
5 C. G. Jung, *Psychology and Religion* (New Haven: Yale University Press, (1938) 1964) par. 520.
6 ibid par. 520.
7 Carl G. Jung, *Mysterium Coniunctionis, CW XIV,* (London: Routledge and Kegan Paul, (1963) 1970). par. 679.
8 John A. Sanford, *Healing and Wholeness*, Copyright © 1977 Paulist Press, New York. 19.
9 T. S. Eliot, *Four Quartets* from *Collected Poems* 1909-1962 (London: Faber and Faber, (1963) 1974) 213
10 Ursula Le Guin, op. cit., 56.

Chapter 7

Inner Marriage: Love and Ecstasy

Keep, then, this entire commandment that I am command-
ing you today, so that you may have strength to go in and
occupy the land that you are crossing over to occupy...the
land you are crossing over to occupy is a land of hills and
valleys watered by rain from the sky, a land that the Lord
your God looks after.

The eyes of the Lord your God are always on it, from
the beginning of the year to the end of the year.

If you will only heed his every commandment that I am
commanding you today — loving the Lord your God, and
serving him with all your heart and with all your soul — then
he will give the rain for your land in its season, the early
rain and the later rain, and you will gather in your grain,
your wine, and your oil....

Dt 11:8, 11-14

In Semitic thought, the human being is seen as a unity and
the word "heart" conveys the whole interior life of the
person. The exhortation of the Old and New Testaments to
love God, neighbour and self with all our heart means we
must love with our whole personality. The whole of our
personality is the marriage of the ego and the Self, experienced through the interplay of the persona and shadow, and
the ego and anima/animus.

Love and responsible choice go hand in hand, and without an integrated personality neither is truly possible. The
strength to love and to journey into the interior land of the
heart comes with God's grace who waters and tends the
soil. Co-operation with the loving, integrating power of
God brings the grain of nourishment, the oil of gladness, the
wine of ecstasy.

The Archetype and Wine of Ecstasy

In Greek mythology, the archetype of ecstasy is found in the god of wine, Dionysius, who represents irrationality, sensation and intuition. In Roman mythology, Dionysius became Bacchus, the god of intoxication. The drunken Bacchus was ousted by Apollo, the god of light, who represents rationality, law and order. In contemporary Western society, the feeling, sensuous and irrational Dionysius needs to come home to consciousness and to show us, once again, how to integrate the masculine and the feminine. To experience ecstasy and its transforming power, we need to welcome what the androgynous Dionysius represents.

The word androgyne comes from *anér* (man) and *gyné* (woman). Dionysius is, in Greek Mythology, the divine androgyne: the god in whom the characteristics of both male and female unite.

In Christian art and iconology, Christ, too, is depicted as a divine androgyne. In him there is no division between male and female (cf Gal 3:28) and, frequently, he is portrayed as a rather feminine man. Jung spoke of the importance of Christ's androgyn since it lays the foundation for the *transcendent function* i.e. the reconciliation of opposites, and the marriage of the masculine and the feminine.

Robert Johnson notes that, "Because we have lost touch with our anima or animus we have lost touch with each other and with the Dionysian principle, which would give us so much of joy and ecstasy if we but knew it."[1] He points out that we all carry the archetype of ecstasy deep within us. This is evident from the increase in addictive behaviour and the growth of the drug culture in Western society. "Addiction", he notes, "is the negative side of spiritual seeking."[2] Unfortunately, addictive behaviour and the eagerness to avoid pain are deadening the transformative power of ecstasy in the Western world. As Johnson so rightly points out, the archetype of ecstasy needs to be lived out with dignity and consciousness. To do this the archetypal Dionysius needs to be invited out of his negative and delusory hiding places. Instead of going down the negative side of spiritual seeking, Dionysius needs to be met with enthusiasm:

> To express ecstasy with dignity and consciousness we must meet it head on, with a joyful spirit of acceptance. Enthusiasm annuls the distance between the pairs of opposites, and this brings ecstatic joy.[3]

To experience ecstasy and the love of God, we must be willing to invite profound change, to enter into a radically altered state of self-awareness. One must be willing to experience deep sorrow as well as ecstatic joy, wounding absence as well as healing presence. The reality of ecstatic love and wounding is brought out in the Biblical love song of Solomon:

> My beloved thrust his hand into the opening,
>   and my inmost being yearned for him.
> I arose to open to my beloved,
>   and my hands dripped with myrrh,
>   my fingers with liquid myrrh,
>   upon the handles of the bolt.
> I opened to my beloved, but my beloved had
>   turned and was gone.
> My soul failed me when he spoke,
>   I sought him but did not find him;
>   I called him, but he gave no answer.
> Making their rounds in the city
>   the sentinels found me;
>   they beat me, they wounded me,
>   they took away my mantle...
>   (Song of Solomon 5:4-7)

The Song of Solomon finds an echo in *The Spiritual Canticle* of St John of the Cross:

Why, since you wounded
this heart, don't you heal it?
And why, since You stole it from me,
do you leave it so,
and fail to carry off what You have stolen? [4]

A conscious choice to stay with the pain of wounding,
rather than falling into the trap of the "quick-fix" mentality,
will eventually lead to moments of ecstatic union and transformation. Love and ecstasy involve a deathlike experience
as Jungian therapist, Linda Schierse Leonard, discovered in
her own life:

> There was, I learned, a dark death in the heart of
> love, a deep death through which I had to let myself
> descend before I could meet with love which was not
> power, before I could meet with love which was
> whole and holy. [5]

This descent demands a death to ego-control, a death to
preconceived notions and prejudices, a death to delusion
and addiction. In the preface to her book, *The Wounded
Woman*, Leonard relates how suddenly her repressed
Dionysian side emerged. In the depths she was confronted
with her own irrationality and with her own drunkenness
and anger. A wild seductive side to her emerged. She
describes the writing of her second book, *On the Way to the
Wedding*, as her ascent from the depths. In this book she
describes her inner obstacles to the wedding as: "the Ghostly
Lover"; "Prince Charming and the Special Princess"; "the
Bewitchment"; "the Demon Lover"; and "the Ring of
Power". [6] In speaking of romantic love, Leonard writes:

> I also drank the "love potion" like Tristan and Isolde.
> I became enchanted by the spell of wine – a potion
> which first brought me the ecstatic longing for the
> winged love that soars eternally, the promise of total

union – a potion which later became a poison for me and threatened death. On the physical level I suffered from the disease of alcoholism... On the emotional level I suffered from a dualism that split life and love off from death, that always sought the eternal realm and avoided the ordinary.[7]

The pathway to the wedding and to ecstatic union cannot bypass the "redness of life". We must come up against the ordinary.

Heterosexual Lovers and Inner Marriage

"Love at first sight" and "love is blind" are familiar sayings in our vocabulary. Both sayings convey an intensity of emotion which, all too frequently, wears off and can become animosity at second sight. The archetypal image of woman in a man's unconscious is the anima, and the archetypal image of man in a woman's unconscious is the animus. Since these archetypal images are unconscious, they are experienced through projections onto the opposite sex. When a heterosexual woman falls in love at first sight, she is really in love with her projected animus and is blinded by the projection. For the heterosexual man, it means falling in love and being blinded by his projected anima. This projection of the contrasexual image is the dynamic not only for heterosexual attraction and mating, but also for repulsion.

The anima and animus belong to the realm of the gods and goddesses in Greek mythology and they can have a powerful, magnetic numinous quality. Falling in love with the projected anima or animus initiates potent life-giving emotion which may lead to experiences of intense rapture and ecstasy. The word ecstasy is derived from *ex stasis* which means to stand outside oneself. It is a transportation into a different realm. Robert A. Johnson notes that,

"Romantic love is the single greatest energy system in the Western psyche. In our culture it has supplanted religion as the arena in which men and women seek meaning, transcendence, wholeness and ecstasy."[8] He goes on to point out that:

> ...our approach to romantic love is not working well. Despite our ecstasy when we are "in love", we spend much of our time with a deep sense of loneliness, alienation, and frustration over our inability to make genuinely loving and committed relationships. Usually we blame other people for failing us; it doesn't occur to us that perhaps it is we who need to change our own unconscious attitudes – the expectations and demands we impose on our relationships and on other people. This is the great wound in the Western psyche.[9]

As John A. Sanford points out, being in love is a matter for the gods, and if we *always* seek the eternal realm of the gods and goddesses by avoiding and denying the ordinary, then our love relationships are in jeopardy.

Sanford describes the anima and animus as the Invisible Partners in every human relationship, and in every person's search for individual wholeness.[10] He notes that these Invisible Partners have a great influence on a relationship. This is so because the person who is carrying the projected image of anima or animus, for the other person, is either highly overvalued or excessively undervalued. The intensity of the projection clouds the human reality of the individual.[11] When a person, in his or her human frailty, fails to live up to the ideal of the projected image, then the intensity of attraction can easily turn into the intensity of repulsion. A good example of anima projection is found in Thomas Hardy's novel, *Tess of the d'Urbervilles*. In this story, Angel Clare, whose name suggests that he has done little to integrate his shadow-side, falls in love with a beautiful but pure image of Tess. On their wedding night Angel confesses a sexual encounter from his past and seeks the forgiveness of Tess. When Tess makes a similar confession Angel declares: "...the woman I have been ~ving is not you". And in reply to Tess' question, "But ~?", he states: "Another woman in your shape". Tess' ~ment and words are heart-rending:

> ~ught, Angel, that you loved me – me, my very
> ~?

~itial stages, the relationship between Angel and ~ ~unded on a powerful anima projection, and as Sanford explains:

> ...to the extent that a relationship is founded on projection, the element of human love is lacking... Real love begins only when one person comes to know another for who he or she really is as a human being, and begins to like and care for that human being.[13]

Angel had to face his own shadow side and withdraw his ideal projected image of woman from Tess before his real love for her could begin. Tragically, however, his real love and acceptance came too late.

It could be argued that, at first, Angel saw his marriage to Tess in terms of well-being: he viewed it as a means to happiness, satisfaction, and self-fulfilment. A healthier, alternative view to marriage is in terms of salvation: marriage is one pathway among others leading to self-knowledge and individuation.[14]

The inner marriage of the masculine and the feminine in each of us has an important impact on relationships in the outer arena of the world. Through this deepening inner marriage, we can progressively withdraw our projections which give rise to jaundiced vision and spoil the hope of authentic relationship and genuine marriage. The inner marriage of masculine and feminine enables us to see others as unique individuals and to lovingly accept their giftedness and limitations. It enables us to put Christ's command not to judge (cf Mt 7:1-5) into practice, and to fulfil his desire and prayer that we be One (cf Jn 17:11). It is interesting to note that Jesus chose the vine for his image of unity. The vine produces the fruit which is crushed until its juices flow to produce wine, the archetype of ecstasy.

Homosexual Lovers and Inner Marriage

Homosexuality is a complex issue and, as John A. Sanford points out, referring to it as a uniform phenomenon is misleading. "In general," he states, "we refer to homosexuality whenever a man has a sexual erotic desire for another male, or for the male organ."[15] He identifies at least three types of homosexual experience among men, two of which can also be experienced by men in heterosexual relationships.

For some men their other side, which typifies wholeness, is not represented by the ideal image of a woman but by the figure of an androgynous, divine youth. In such instances, it is the unconscious Self which is being projected onto the other person rather than the anima. Very often a younger man will carry this projection of the Self for an older man and in essence it is a desire for integration and wholeness. Conversely, an older man may carry the projected Self for a younger man. In this instance the older man typifies the power and authority of the Self: the figure of the positive father.[16]

In the above types of homosexuality the object of desire is another male. There is also a type of homosexuality which has the male organ as its object of desire, and as Sanford states: "Often such a yearning represents symbolically a deep need for connection with the Self, represented by the phallus, symbol of the creative masculine spirit".[17]

In other types of homosexuality the anima does play a

dominant role but in the ego psychology of the man. This is the type of homosexuality which gives rise to the notion that all homosexuals are effeminate men. In such instances the man does not identify his ego with masculinity, and there is an overidentification with the anima which produces a feminized male ego. Instead of a marriage taking place between ego-consciousness and the anima, there occurs a kind of fusion. In this type of homosexuality it is the man's undeveloped masculinity which is projected onto the other male.[18]

Similarly, overidentification with the animus can give rise to a type of lesbianism among women. If a woman identifies with the masculine Logos principle which is spirit, then she will project her undeveloped Eros principle, which is bodily and incarnate, onto another woman. In essence she is projecting her desire to be grounded in the Self.

Regardless of sexual orientation, we are all called to wholeness which is symbolized by the divine androgyne and the inner sacred marriage of the masculine and the feminine. As already stated, personality is fidelity to the law of one's being and it is everybody's desire to develop it.

In Ignatian spirituality the *Id Quod Volo* (i.e. what one "desires") is extremely important. It is assumed that, at the deepest level of the individual, God's desire and the individual's desire are one. This desire is for integration, wholeness and ecstatic union. Unfortunately, sexual fantasies and sexual desires have been almost totally denigrated in some Christian circles, when, in fact, they hold the key to wholeness and holiness. As John A. Sanford states: "As a rule of thumb, it can be said that what we yearn for sexually is a symbolic representation of what we need in order to become whole."[19]

Celibate Lovers and Inner Marriage

June Singer makes the important distinction between celibacy which is freely chosen and celibacy which is imposed from without. If celibacy takes the form of mere virginity which denies the sexual nature of the individual and demands that he or she transcend this nature, then this celibate state has no virtue. Imposed celibacy too frequently springs from a belittling view of sexuality; a view which sees sexuality, as Singer notes, as an impediment to the commitment and devotion required by the religious life. If celibacy is to bear fruit, it must be freely chosen and sexual:

> Sexuality does not always require a partner. It can be experienced as inner union. There is a form of celibacy which is highly sexual. By this I mean the energies of love can be fully experienced by one who is alone. In the alembic of one's own body it is possible to produce a rare and precious substance. This is the result of freely choosing celibacy as a way of life.[20]

This rare and precious substance is the product of the inner marriage of masculine and feminine energies, of the active and receptive.

To experience the energies of love within, one must, in fact, engage in what John Perkins calls symbolic incest. Perkins distinguishes between inner symbolic incest and outer literal incest. Symbolic incest is an interpersonal relationship; it is the archetypal integration of the whole personality and is potentially creative. The integration of the whole personality is symbolically incestuous because the anima is the inner mother-sister-daughter and the animus is the inner father-brother-son. On the other hand literal incest is an interpersonal relationship; a destructive "acting out" of the archetype. As Perkins notes there is an extroverted reason and an introverted reason for the incest taboo. The introverted or spiritual purpose is to redirect a certain portion of love and sexuality back toward its source in the unconscious. This results in the awareness of an inner erotic image, the anima or animus, and of transpersonal reality:

This, Perkins states, is precisely the deeper purpose of the age-old ideals of chastity and celibacy the world over. Here outward expression of unrestrained sexuality is curtailed in order to produce a heightened and protected awareness of erotic energy inwardly... [Incest] is "horrible" when it functions between people and "sacred" when it functions *within* people.[21]

Archetypal celibacy is grounded in inner sexual relatedness, in interior intercourse with the contrasexual. However, this is not the ultimate goal or the fullest experience of love since the inner marriage gives birth to the Self.

John Perkins notes that symbolic incest is primarily a religious phenomenon because the Latin *religio* means to unite what has been fragmented. Therefore, religion is related to a "holiness" which is a true "wholeness".[22] John Welch makes the important distinction between the androgyne which symbolizes union of the two modes of human personality, and the spiritual marriage which symbolizes the union of that personality with God. Both, however, are interrelated. It would seem that the spiritual marriage assumes an androgynous person, and that the spiritual marriage symbolizes both the wedding of the human and the divine; and the marriage of the ego and the anima or animus.[23] God calls us into the wholeness of our identity wherein lies our unique individuality and our freedom for ecstatic union with God.

A wholesome celibate will flow with the rhythm of life, energized by the interplay between the masculine and the feminine. John P. Dourley describes this inner love affair as "a sacrament of the Self" and "as the gateway to an even more extensive love of reality beyond [the individual]".[24]

Both the wholesome and unwholesome celibate have to pay a price for their respective states. The unwholesome celibate is cut off from the deep spring of life and love; from the integrating energy of his or her deepest truth; from the spring which wells up to eternal life and ecstatic union with

God. The resulting inner void tends to fill with the darkness and despair of meaninglessness, the blackness of depression, the weight of lethargy and, if the person does not begin to listen to the unconscious and enter into partnership with it, the lifeless inner void will manifest itself in the secondary process of physical illness. However, this inner void may well be the very place where he or she hears the personal call to wholeness and holiness, to love and to ecstasy. It is possible for the person said to be barren to become pregnant with new life (cf Lk 1:36).

To become a wholesome celibate the individual must pass through the barren inner desert and descend into the depths of the *nigredo*. He or she must come face to face with sensuality and with the power of instinctuality which registers in bodily urges. The celibate will be confronted with the temptation to exteriorize eros and to act out his or her sexuality. In the *nigredo*, or in the dark night of the senses, the sensory appetites, gratifications and supports enter a death process so that the integrating divine spark, the living flame of love might dance into life. It is important to stress that this is a *process*. Western Christian spirituality still fails to fully grasp the point that spirit is encountered in a process which is worked out in the body and the soul.

The call to a celibate lifestyle may be experienced as a wounding: a wounding which is both caused and healed by the living flame of love. It is a death-like wounding, but death changes to life when we allow divine energy to flow through the wound. This energy and life coming from the unconscious is the gift of hidden manna (cf Ex 16; Rev 2:17). It is the source of nourishment for the journey through life; for the journey toward wholeness and holiness, love and ecstasy; for the journey toward the white stone with one's new name written on it.

A New Name For All

Whatever an individual's sexual orientation and whatever the concrete expression of that orientation in a chosen lifestyle – whether celibate or non-celibate – each individual is called by *name* and is loved by God. Each individual is journeying towards the engraved white stone with his or her secret name and deepest identity. Each individual is on the way to the wedding:

> Whether one lives the wedding in an outer relationship, in work in the world, or in a meditative life, it is the transformation within that provides the transcendent ground of the wedding.[25]

A Meditative Life

We engage in "sacred" incest when we meditate and contemplate.[26] Intuition, which is connected with Dionysian irrationality and ecstasy, "is cultivated by meditation, which opens the person to the influx of that which is beyond ego. Meditation... is a way of tending the fire... [of concentrating] on the flickering movement of the flame within, burning at all times."[27]

Once discerned, our *personal vocation* may be used as a mantra to tend the divine fire within. Contemplation of our own secret name may sound rather self-centred but it is that sacred incestuous act which holds the secret of unity and integration for the individual. It is that sacred incestuous act which "puts on" Christ, our brother, and opens the individual at the core of his or her being so that the transcendent God may be encountered. It may be called the *anagoge* or elevating process which restores us to a unitive state with God. The recitation of our *personal vocation* may act as a *motus anagogicus*, i.e. an anagogical or bridging movement, bridging the island (ego-identity) with the large hinterland (unconscious identity) and bringing the opposites ever closer together.

The myth of Echo has been used to illustrate the dynamics of mantra prayer. In this myth Echo acts as a distraction to Hera so that Zeus can go philandering. Underneath the repetition and echoing of the mantra there is something much deeper going on. The mind, like Hera, needs to be distracted to give the soul space and to give God space in the individual's life. The repetition of the mantra brings a stillness to the activity of the mind and glimpses of the inner, deeper Self which is beyond ego-consciousness. The aim of mantra-type prayer is integration and unity: the integration of the human being – body, soul and spirit – and union with God. Mantra-type prayer echoes more and more deeply in the depths of one's being, helping the individual to "put on" the inner Self, to put on the inner Christ.

Putting on Christ leads to new vision, and new vision amounts to a loving recognition of our paradoxical wholeness. It is an ongoing, dynamic unfolding: an opening out to the divine initiative which is symbolized in the metaphor of marriage. In his summary of the unitive way, in the spiritual tradition, Thomas D. McGonigle O.P. states:

> Although the ecstatic prayer of betrothal is transitory, the individual senses that he or she has been given a new heart and that, in truth, it is Christ who is the deepest reality at the centre of one's being and activity.[28]

In Jungian terms, this is the encounter between the ego and the Self and the movement toward the Self as the new psychic centre.

In *The Interior Castle*, St Teresa of Avila uses the image of a diamond, or clear crystal, to represent the individual, and she describes the journey of the soul through six dwelling places until it reaches the Centre where Christ, the King, dwells. In this seventh dwelling place, the individual experiences a vision of Christ and a spiritual union against the backdrop of the Trinity's presence. Is this imaginative vision of Christ, which heralds spiritual union, the "face" of Christ Jesus which is proper to each individual? – the face of Christ Jesus which is the integrating and unifying force in a person's life...the treasure buried in the field...the pearl of great price?

St John of the Cross, in his writings, speaks of the substantial word which rises from the depth and centre of the soul. This deep centre is where truth resides and where the human and divine caress and penetrate. In a similar vein, St Ignatius of Loyola made a distinction between interior words which arise from the depths of the psyche and exterior words which come from a more superficial layer. Is the substantial word of John's writings and the interior word of Ignatius' writings found in the theme of *personal vocation*? Is the substantial word or the interior word that secret name written on the white stone...that secret name which reveals itself in an ever deepening light...that name which holds the secret of love and ecstatic union?

Summary

Divine mating and archetypal androgyn inspire our journey to sacred ground; our journey to the divine integrating spark within and to ecstatic union. Staying on this journey, however, requires that we carry our own baggage and that we withdraw our shadow projections from other people. It also requires the issuing of a conscious invitation to the divine androgyne, and a desire for a deepening inner marriage with our "Invisible Partners". It is this deepening inner marriage – which is nourished by a meditative life, and may be lived in an outer relationship or in a celibate state – which will lead us to a love that endures; to a love which is whole and holy; to a love which cannot be explained because it belongs to the realm of mystery.

NOTES

1 Robert A. Johnson, *Ecstasy: Understanding the Psychology of Joy* Copyright © 1987 Harper & Row, San Francisco. 39.

2 ibid vii.

3 ibid 52.

4 K. Kavanaugh O.C.D. & O. Rodriguez O.C.D., eds., op. cit., 443.

5 From *On the Way to the Wedding* by Linda Schierse Leonard, © 1986. Reprinted by arrangement with Shambhala Publications, Inc., Boston. 192.

6 ibid 10.

7 ibid 191/192.

8 Robert A. Johnson, *We: Understanding the Psychology of Romantic Love* Copyright © 1983 Harper & Row. xi.

9 ibid xii.

10 John A. Sanford, *The Invisible Partners* Copyright © 1980 Paulist Press, New York/Mahwah. 18; 6.

11 ibid 13.

12 Thomas Hardy, *Tess of the d'Urbervilles* (London: Macmillan, 1891, 1975) 255.

13 John A. Sanford, *The Invisible Partners*, 19.

14 Cf ibid 81.

15 Cf ibid 94.

16 Cf ibid 94/95.

17 Cf ibid 96.

18 Cf ibid 98/99.

19 Cf ibid 89.

20 June Singer, *Love's Energies* (Boston: Sigo Press, 1990) 292/293.

21 John Perkins, *The Forbidden Self* (Boston & London: Shambhala, 1992) 39/40.

22 Cf ibid 45.

23 Cf John Welch, *Spiritual Pilgrims: Carl Jung and Teresa of Avila*, Copyright © 1982 Paulist Press, New York. 183/184.

24 John P. Dourley, *Love, Celibacy and the Inner Marriage* (Toronto: Inner City Books, 1987) 41.

25 From *On the Way to the Wedding* by Linda Schierse Leonard, © 1986. Reprinted by arrangement with Shambhala Publications, Inc., Boston. 10.

26 John Perkins, op. cit., 40. Perkins also includes the following in the sacred incestuous act: participation in the symbolic liturgy, attention to one's dreams and the workings of imagination, dialogue with one's own ambivalence and inner conflicts, refusal to contaminate the surrounding world with one's projected fantasies and prejudices.

27 June Singer, op. cit., 288/289.

28 Thomas D. McGonigle O.P., Union, Unitive Way in Michael Downey, ed., *The New Dictionary of Catholic Spirituality* (Collegeville, Minnesota: Liturgical Press, 1993) 987-988 at 987.

Chapter 8

Synthesis: Personal Vocation and Personal Myth

Here the impossible union
Of spheres of existence is actual...
T.S. Eliot, *The Dry Salvages, Four Quartets*

Both Carl G. Jung and Herbert Alphonso S.J. are concerned with the dynamic process which unfolds an individual's incomparable uniqueness. This incomparable uniqueness, they maintain, holds the secret of personal meaning and of integrated, wholesome living. For Alphonso, one's *personal vocation* is the secret of unity and integration at the heart of a whole life. Psychologically speaking the *personal vocation* may be described as the *transcendent function*: that personal reconciling symbol which draws us ever closer to the Symbol, the eternal Word. For Jung, one's personal myth and the process of individuation is the secret of the inner marriage between the masculine and the feminine, that sacred marriage which enables a person to sustain the inner and outer dialectic of life.

The experience of vocation or call is an important feature for both writers. This call comes from a power beyond ego-identity. Alphonso names this power God, and Jung, as a psychologist, names this power the unconscious which acts like the law of God. The law of our being, i.e. our deepest Self and incomparable uniqueness, is, they both maintain, present from the mother's womb. This deep, inner law has the teleological function to manifest itself in each individual's life, to write itself into our concrete history.

Alphonso believes that we are made in the image of God and that our deepest Self is a God-image. More precisely, he believes that this soul-image is a "face" of Christ Jesus which is proper to each individual and which manifests itself in a unique animating spirit. For Jung, the Self cannot be distinguished from a God-image but, as a psychologist, he speaks of Christ being a symbol of the Self. As a theologian Alphonso would hold that the Self is a symbol of Christ, Christ being a living, transcendent reality. Consequently, the relationship with the Self transcends intrapsychic relatedness, and this is the arena of theology and not that of psychology. From Jung's psychological perspective, the aetiology of the Self is rooted in an archetype; from the viewpoint of theology and Christian spirituality it is rooted in the transcendent God. This is where both disciplines diverge. Jung's depth psychology emphasizes the *imprint*; Christian spirituality also stresses the *imprint* but is not afraid to acknowledge the *imprinter* and to name the *imprinter* as the transcendent God. As Ann B. Ulanov states:

> Depth psychology again and again comes to a stop at its own borders. It is able only then to point beyond itself. It can tell us a great deal about how...images live in us, embody our longings, and how our pictures of God function for our health or illness. But surely we want more than this... We want to know if our God-image speaks of God as well as ourselves. We want to see, hear, touch, penetrate, receive that Other, that holy Other, who lives objectively as an independent subject, standing over against us, reaching out to us, who changes our whole way of perceiving the gap between us and the divine by crossing over to us from the other side... It is only religion, theology, the Church's life that dares to go beyond this boundary-line of depth psychology, to brave the unknown waters...[1]

Our personal myth and *personal vocation* share the same

common ground, but our *personal vocation* takes us a step further into a relationship with the transcendent yet immanent God. We meet God within the reality of our own story and of our own concrete history; within the context of being body-soul-spirit people. The creation narratives in the Book of Genesis imply that the primary vocation from God is to become a human being: the best human being possible. Every other call or vocation builds on this initial call. Alphonso does not make this point explicitly – a point which is reinforced by the Incarnation – and, therefore, Jung's depth psychology throws much needed light on the human journey. God, through the person of Jesus Christ, is at home in our humanness; and, first and foremost, we are called to be at home in our human condition with all its limitations. To accept our humanity and to live out the consequences of this God-given gift is integral to Christianity. If we are to discover our divine spark within, we must lovingly accept the humanity entrusted to us. To be true to ourselves we must be obedient to our destiny as body-soul-spirit people; i.e. we must have a listening heart which does not attempt to exclude any part of our God-given personality.

A synthesis of *personal vocation* and personal myth challenges us to reflect anew on the Incarnation. The Incarnation is, indeed, the gift half understood.

The primary vocation from God to become the best human being possible is a call to inner marriage and wholeness, a call to unity and integration. Our *personal vocation* is our unique God-given way of experiencing the *coniunctio*, of holding the inner and outer dialectics of life in creative tension. This is an internal and an external marriage. It is a marriage of nature and of grace, of the human and the divine, of the masculine and the feminine, of psychology and of spirituality.

The giving of the white stone with a new name is a symbol of the most complete individuation possible and of the highest ecstatic transformation: it symbolizes being "oned" within, being "oned" with others and being "oned" with the transcendent God:

You shall be called by a new name...
and your land shall be married (Is 62:2b;4c).

NOTES

1   Ann Belford Ulanov, *The Wisdom of the Psyche* (Cambridge, Massachusetts: Cowley Pub., 1988) 18.

Part Two
Praxis

Introduction

So how do we discover our own inner path
to find out who we were meant to be?
To this question there is no general answer.
The singularity of each of our paths is part of
what makes finding it and staying on it so difficult.
Lawrence W. Jaffe, Liberating the Heart

The God-given uniqueness of each individual means that there is no set way for finding the curved, spiralling pathway of one's *personal vocation* and personal myth: the "Way" is as varied as our multifaceted and mysterious God. Additionally, *personal vocation* and personal myth are a dynamic process and each individual will have his or her own way of staying within the dynamic or of sabotaging it.

Lawrence Jaffe does suggest, however, two collective truths which may be helpful to hold, or even cling to, on this journey of discovery and rediscovery:

Remember that God wants to incarnate in you... Another way to say it is that your desire to become who you were meant to be is a powerful instinct which you must find a way to serve... You must give expression to what is most truly yourself. For instance, you may need to write or paint or work in the garden or sail or play tennis or change your profession or love someone even if it makes a fool of you.[1]

St Irenaeus said that the glory of God is a person fully alive. We are most fully alive when we give expression to our deepest and truest Self. Lawrence Jaffe suggests that taking a Sabbath, i.e. a time of rest, may be a valid general precept for serving God and the individuation process. He points out the importance of (a) protecting this Sabbath from the claims of others; (b) trying to be open to whatever comes in this free, protected time; and (c) being regular in taking this Sabbath time:

> Take a Sabbath, a time of rest, once a week even if only for fifteen minutes. Protect this Sabbath from the claims of work, children, spouse, parents and friends. When you enter your free and protected space for those minutes try to be open to what comes to you. You can think of it as a meditation if you want, or perhaps you will feel the urge to write or paint or draw or dance or think or be sad or be angry or be in nature. Regularity in taking your Sabbath is essential, however, so body and soul will come to anticipate it and depend upon it.[2]

Sabbath time is a time of space; a time of silence; a time of listening to the depths of our being; a time of expressing those very depths where we are our ownmost selves, made in the image and likeness of God. *Sabbath time* is engaging in that sacred incestuous act which may take any shape from meditation to art work to symbolic liturgy to dreamwork to inner dialogue etc.[3]

The following chapters, in this synthesis, are not intended to be prescriptive answers in the quest for one's unique pathway in life. Rather, they offer practical suggestions for *Sabbath time*, which may aid the unfolding fabric and fire of one's *personal vocation* and personal myth. There is no magical formula or exercise. There is encounter.

NOTES

1 Lawrence W. Jaffe, *Liberating the Heart* (Toronto: Inner City Books, 1990) 88.
2 ibid 88/89.
3 Cf John Perkins, op. cit., 40.

Chapter 9

Take Your Pen for a Walk

Tonight I took the leash off my pen.
At first it was frightened,
looked up at me with confused eyes, tongue panting.
Then I said, Go on, run away,
and pushed its head.
Still it wasn't sure what I wanted;
it whimpered with its tail between its legs.
So I yelled, You're free, why don't you run
you stupid pen, you should be glad.
Now get out of my sight.
It took a few steps.
I stamped my foot and threw a stone.
Suddenly, it realised what I was saying
and began to run furiously away from me.

Julie O'Callaghan

The above poem by Julie O'Callaghan expresses a desire to walk and run freely in the field of creativity. It also conveys the frustration felt when creative energies are blocked, and that fear we might feel when we are suddenly faced with freedom.

Often we live our lives in a zone of entrapment rather than in a zone of surging, flowing creative energy. We need to let go of persona ideals and egotistical points of view and invite our creative Centre to express itself. Taking our pen for a walk across the pages of a journal, without imposing censorship on any thoughts and feelings, is one way of giving our core, creative Self the space to express itself.

Ira Progoff and the Intensive Journal Method

The keeping of personal journals, or diaries, is a widespread and age-old practice, but Dr Ira Progoff is the father of the *Intensive Journal* method which came to a systematic birth in 1966. He realised the limitations of the traditional type of journal which usually takes the shape of a record of chronological events in the person's life. From his own personal experience, and his experience as a psychotherapist, he developed a structured, integrative format for journalling.

The *Intensive Journal* method is a system of writing techniques which aid the process of personal awareness, growth and development by incorporating a dynamic of feedback for the individual. It is a method which brings the individual's whole life into focus and reveals his or her lifelines or life-patterns. It draws a person's life toward wholeness and holiness by building a bridge between the individual's inner life and outer life. It does this in keeping with the rhythm and beat of the individual's soul and it helps to connect us with that underlying and unifying reality which is our unique and personal source of meaning. The *Intensive Journal* method helps us to discover the connective thread which is woven into our concrete history and which carries the meaning of our lives. This connective thread is the guiding, integrating force of our God-given name and our inner personal myth.

Journal Workshop

Ira Progoff recommends attendance at a Journal Workshop as the most effective way to begin the journalling process. Attendance at a Journal Workshop is shared *Sabbath time* with other people. It is a sacred space in the midst of life's activity where the individual enjoys both privacy and group support.

Attendance at a Journal Workshop brings two main achievements: (a) we experience the movement of our lives as a whole. This happens by drawing past and present experiences into focus against the canvas of future possibilities and potential; and (b) we learn the technique of the Journal Feedback method which enables us to use the Journal workbook effectively on our own.

The Integrative Structure of the Journal Workbook

The Journal workbook has two main divisions: (a) the Log sections and (b) the Feedback sections.

The Log sections gather the raw experiences of our lives and they have a basic factual role. In this section we record the facts and experiences of our lives, as objectively as possible, without censorship, judgement or interpretation.

Journal work begins with the Period Log where we focus on the stretchable NOW of our lives. This NOW is not a static moment but a unit of flowing time in which we find ourselves. The NOW of our lives is "our most recent relevant past as it moves into our present".[1] The period that is NOW is unique to the individual and will vary in length according to each person. The description of our inner and outer experiences, in this NOW of our lives, forms the base and context of our journal work.

Exercise: Getting in touch with the Now
• Get into a comfortable body posture, close your eyes and relax. It may be helpful to use some relaxation techniques such as breathing exercises, or the tensing and relaxing of muscles throughout the body.
• Be open to feeling the movement of your life. Give deliberate thinking a rest!
• Ask yourself the question, "Where am I now in my life?", but feel the implications of the question. Do not

analyse. Feel the movement of your life as it is taking shape in the present.

• Let spontaneous, descriptive answers to the question rise up. A simile or metaphor may come to you to describe this period. Briefly record what comes to you in the Period Log. It may be helpful to start by writing,

My life in this period is like ....
or
My life in this period has been ....

For example, somebody might use a simile such as, "My life in this period is like a lifting fog"; or, "My life in this period is like a hard mountain climb"; or somebody might use a metaphor by saying, "My life in this period is (or has been) a barren desert"; or, "My life in this period is (or has been) a green pasture with springs of fresh, living water." The important thing is to let the descriptive movement and shape of this period, in your life, rise to consciousness.

• This imaging of the NOW period in our lives is a preparatory step for looking at the contents of this period in more detail. You might use the following as a starting point,

This is a time in my life when ....

The following pointers are helpful in entering the detailed contents of the period:
• When did this stretchable NOW period begin? Is there a significant event or happening connected with its beginning? Perhaps the beginning of this period can be identified with a particular memory of previous events?

• When the boundaries of this NOW period have been established, reconstruct the outline of the period by recalling any significant and specific details pertaining to:

- Events
- Relationships
- Work activities
- Social activities
- Inner experiences
- Dream experiences

Twilight Imaging

When we have searched our memories and written our basic entry into the Period Log, Progoff then suggests a time of stillness. This time of stillness is intended to aid a shift in our psychic position from the conscious, rational level to the nonrational, intuitive depths. This different psychic approach to the NOW of our lives is facilitated by Twilight Imaging. Twilight Imaging is another name for what Carl Jung called active imagination, and it takes place in that borderline state between waking and sleeping. We consciously allow images and perceptions to rise spontaneously from the unconscious, and we follow their movements without allowing our conscious reason to interfere. The imagery and perceptions of this twilight experience are recorded in the Twilight Imagery Log under the heading Period Image – again without judgement or interpretation.

The NOW of our lives has now been approached from the standpoint of rational consciousness and from the symbolic point of view. It is important to consider the relationship between these two viewpoints. Does the symbolic point of view confirm or contradict rational consciousness? Do both standpoints complement each other? "When we set the two together," as Progoff explains, "the outer and inner perceptions combine to enable us to perceive the organic wholeness of time as it is moving in our lives."[2]

This work in the Period Log helps to position ourselves in the dynamic movement of our lives. We find ourselves in a space between the past and the unfolding future, and we gain a broad perspective of the pathway of our lives and where it is trying to lead us.

Daily Log

Recording our current experiences in the Daily Log keeps us in touch with the larger, unfolding movement of our lives. This is where we record our subjective experiences of the day which form the source material for the Feedback dynamic. Progoff distinguishes two main ways of working in the Daily Log: (a) by using recapitulation, or, (b) by using current recording. The process of recapitulation treats the day as a unit and it involves remembering and recreating the events of the day at its close. The method of current recording involves the writing of experiences as they happen during the day.

The data which is recorded in the Log sections is then channelled into the Feedback sections where active exercises transform the material into a dynamic movement of experience. These inner movements of experience are the focus of Progoff's journalling method.

The method distinguishes three main types of inner movement which take place simultaneously:

(a) the Life/Time Dimension;
(b) the Dialogue Dimension;
(c) the Depth Dimension.

The Life/Time Dimension

The Life/Time dimension holds our life history and our unique, personal story or myth. Working in the Life/Time dimension stretches us beyond the NOW of our lives and progressively builds a broader perspective of our whole, and unfolding, story.

Working with the Intensive Journal process is like loosening the soil of our lives, so that our inner land can have its wedding and be fertile. As Progoff explains, our experiences can pile up leaving our lives like hard, untilled soil under the pressure of events. Working with the journal process is like a gentle plough breaking into the hardness of our lives, creating space for the fresh air of awareness. It can nurture the seed of our deep, inner self, and bring about a new and richer unit of existence.[3]

The Intensive Journal process brings about a growth in interior freedom. We begin to venture into unexplored caves. We get the courage to shine a light on the dark corners in ourselves. We experience the lightness to play with the sand of our lives. We get the strength and energy to hold our mixed experiences, and to build and be creative. We become more flexible, more pliant in the potter's hands (cf Jer 18:1-7).

The flexible movement of our lives is helped by, what Progoff calls, Time-Stretching exercises. Time-Stretching takes us beyond the linear or chronological dimension of time and we are enabled to reach back and forth; to touch and enter different units of time. In a sense we enter a different, interior time zone which Progoff distinguishes as qualitative, rather than linear or chronological. This interplay between the different segments of time/life reveals a pattern of interrelated threads and of divergent threads; and future possibilities and implications come to view in a more focused light.

The Life/Time dimension in the journal process invites us to work simultaneously in three different sections:

(a) Steppingstones;
(b) Life History Log;
(c) Intersections: Roads taken and not taken.

Working simultaneously in these sections has the result of widening the range of interplay between the different segments of time/life.

Progoff invites us to begin by looking at the significant points of movement – whether upward or downward, pleasant or painful – on our journey through life, and to list them in the Steppingstones section. This helps us to reconstruct the main movement of our lives and to see the connective threads which carry a sense of meaning and purpose for us as unique individuals. By reconstructing the steppingstones of our past, we are enabled to take a better step into the future.

The steppingstones which we list are signposts, or markers, pointing to different periods of time in our lives. These periods, or units, of time hold various events and experiences, and we are invited to gradually explore each Steppingstone period, beginning with the most significant one in the whole movement. The following areas are important pointers for the brief exploration of these periods:

1. *People*: significant people and relationships in this particular period of my life.

2. *Works*: outer activities and projects either completed or left incomplete; or perhaps planned but never materialised.

3. *Body*: the physical aspect of my life in this period e.g. health, illness, sexuality, sensuality, exercise, etc.

4. *Society*: my relationships with groups or institutions – familial, religious, political, racial or national; historical events; cultural or artistic experiences.

5. *Events*: personal events which were unexpected, sad or happy, or particularly trying, perhaps.

6. *Dreams*: any striking dream or dreams from this period.

7. *Twilight Imagery*: waking visions in this period or any symbols which rose spontaneously from the unconscious.

8. *Wisdom*: any profound insights from this particular period, or any gems of wisdom received.

9. *Intersections*: the directions or decisions I took.

This checklist is a guide for briefly recording the exp/ ences of a period in life and it is progressively expanded in the other relevant sections of the Journal workbook.

While gradually moving through our various Stepping-stone periods, we are simultaneously adding our memories of the past to our Life History Log, and we are exploring the seeds of potential in the unlived aspects of our lives. We do this in the section of the journal, Intersections: Roads Taken and Not Taken. In the poem, 'The Road Not Taken', Robert Frost has captured the moment of coming to a crossroad in life:

> Two roads diverged in a yellow wood,
>   And sorry I could not travel both
>   And be one traveller, long I stood
> And looked down one as far as I could
>   To where it bent in the undergrowth;
>   Then took the other, as just as fair,
>   And having perhaps the better claim,
> Because it was grassy and wanted wear;
>   Though as for that, the passing there
> Had worn them really about the same,
>
>   And both that morning equally lay
>   In leaves no step had trodden black.
>   Oh, I kept the first for another day!
> Yet knowing how way leads on to way,
> I doubted if I should ever come back.
>
>   I shall be telling this with a sigh
>   Somewhere ages and ages hence:
> Two roads diverged in a wood, and I –
>   I took the one less travelled by,
> And that has made all the difference.

As Progoff points out, journal work enables us to retravel the road of our life and to stand, once again, at the crossroads. In a literal sense the road not taken is now beyond reach of our step, but in a symbolic sense it is still walkable, and its hidden potential awaits us. Progoff stresses that these untaken roads are not dead-ends for us, but that they have simply gone underground and can re-emerge with their seeds of potential, opening up new pathways and avenues for the future.

Using our Steppingstone entries as a hinge, we can now stretch time into the past and into the future. We can move backward and forward between our past experiences, recorded in the Life History Log, and our future possibilities, stemming from the exercise on Intersections: Roads Taken and Not Taken.

The data which we gather in the Life/Time section serves as a starting point for the active exercises in the Feedback sections of the Dialogue Dimension and the Depth Dimension.

Dialogue Dimension

In the Life/Time sections we have recorded the experiences of our life history, and now we enter into a dialogical relationship with them. We allow these experiences to speak to us and we write the dialogue scripts in the relevant sections of the Journal workbook. The dialogue dimension establishes an interior relationship with people, experiences and events. We are encouraged to have interior dialogues with the people in our lives; with our various works, activities or projects; with our body; with society; with events; with our dreams, images and symbols; and with our inner wisdom.

Exercise: Dialogue with Persons
– Make a list of people – either living or dead – who have an inner importance for you. Relationships of inner importance will have an emotional pull on you, whether that emotion is positive or negative. In making your list, focus

on the relationships of inner importance which you feel have some unfinished business, perhaps, or are in need of some clarification or further developments.

– In drawing up the list of names, it may be helpful to glance at the entries you have already made in your Journal. The Steppingstones section may connect you with significant people from the past, for example, and the Period Log and Daily Log with significant people from the present.

– Choose a person from the list who feels, to you, to be of current significance in your life. The person may be somebody from the past or the present.

– Write the person's name at the top of the page in your Journal, and date it. Then, sit in silence and concentrate on the person. Consider your relationship in a general way, and feel the tone and quality of the relationship without analysing and going into details.

– Write a short, direct and spontaneous account to describe the essence of the relationship. Indicate, without detail, the movement of the relationship and what phases it has gone through; its positive and negative aspects; what has been satisfying and what has been frustrating; and how the relationship is in the present, including any hopes or anxieties for the future (this is relevant whether the person is living or dead, or from the distant past or present).

– When you have written the account, read it back. If you want to make changes, don't change your original description but add to it.

– The next step is to establish a deep dialogue with the other person. To do this you must place yourself inside the reality of the other person's life. This is helped by reconstructing the person's life and listing his or her Steppingstones. Put yourself in the other person's shoes and write "I" was born... etc.

– When this exercise is completed, Progoff then suggests a time of stillness to allow the spontaneous movement of Twilight Imagery. The perceptions of this time are added to the person's Steppingstones.

– Stay in this twilight atmosphere and feel the presence of the other person and the movement of life.

– Greet the other person, and allow a dialogue to develop. Write down whatever is being said between you and this person.

I: " .... "

N: " .... "

Let the dialogue flow spontaneously. Don't create it deliberately.

– When you have written the dialogue script return to stillness and become aware of the emotions you felt when writing it. Record these emotions, without judgement, as an addition to the dialogue.

– Then read back over the dialogue script in silence and note the emotions which are now rising. Are they the same or different? Record your observations.

– You may find it helpful to read the dialogue script out loud as further feedback.

– If anything occurs in daily life which is connected to this relationship, record it after the dialogue experience in the Journal. As Progoff states, "We fill [the dialogue relationship] in with the flesh and blood of daily reality as we work with it in the continuity of our Journal entries and exercises."[4] Our daily reality is the arena of the "redness" of life. This is where we live out our paradoxical wholeness and incarnate the insights gained.

When we enter into dialogue with our works, body, society and events we follow a similar pattern to that outlined above for dialogue with persons. We make a list; we choose from the list to begin our dialogue work; we write a brief statement about that with which we have chosen to work; we list its Steppingstones or phases of development; we enter a time of stillness and Twilight Imagery which facilitates deep dialogue; we speak and let the "other" speak

116

to us; we record the spontaneous dialogue which takes place; we take note of any feelings or emotions which arose while we were writing the dialogue script; when we reread the dialogue script we take note of any further observations, thoughts and feelings.

Depth Dimension

Working with the dialogue exercises draws us to a level which is deeper than consciousness. We are drawn beyond the surface layer of our lives into the Depth Dimension. Moving into the Depth Dimension involves working with our dreams since they can be unselfconscious reflectors, carrying the seed-nature of a person and his or her goals.

In Progoff's *Intensive Journal* workbook there are two sections for dreamwork: the Dream Log and Dream Enlargements. Progoff advocates a non-analytical way of working with dreams. In the Dream Log we are to record our dream experiences without analysis or interpretation. Then we are encouraged to read a series of our dreams until we feel we are within their movement and carried along by them. Progoff calls this process Twilight Dreaming and we record our thoughts, feelings, insights or intuitions in the Dream Enlargement section. The *Intensive Journal* process is concerned with the unfolding of dreams and their direction rather than with analysis. Dreams and dreamwork will be discussed again in chapter 11.

In addition to dreams and dreamwork, Inner Wisdom Dialogue also helps us to tap into the potentials of knowledge hidden in the depths of our being. This exercise takes us into the spiritual realm, and it is a quest for the meaning and purpose of life and for the ultimate truths of human existence.

– Make a spontaneous list of the Steppingstones of your spiritual life, i.e. of your inner quest for wisdom.

– Give this spontaneous list an approximate chronological order by giving each Steppingstone a number, e.g.

2. *The smell of incense and the ritual procession filled me with a sense of awe and I felt drawn to worship God.*
1. *I felt God was always watching me to catch me doing wrong.*
3. *A piece of music by Bach took me beyond myself and I sensed a greater reality.*

– Read your list in chronological sequence by following your numbering and feel the movement of these Steppingstones. Take note of any feelings or responses which rise for you and record them after your list.

– Think of the people who were of deep significance, for you, during each of these Steppingstone periods. These people may belong to one of two categories: personal wisdom figures and transpersonal wisdom figures. Personal wisdom figures belong to our world and may range from authors, artists, and other public figures to family members. Transpersonal wisdom figures belong to history and the universe. They may be great figures from the past such as Jesus or Buddha; or they may be figures in legend and mythology. Add the name or names of these people to the relevant Steppingstones. Each of these figures or individuals represents an aspect of wisdom for you.

– Choose one of these wisdom figures from your list, either personal or transpersonal, to begin your inner wisdom dialogue.

– Sit in silence with your eyes closed and feel the presence of the wisdom figure you have chosen. Let images rise spontaneously. Greet the wisdom figure and tell him or her what you feel about the quality and wisdom of his or her life. Talk about your own concerns and questions. Write what you say as part of your dialogue script. Wait in silence and let the wisdom figure speak when he or she is ready. Let the dialogue unfold and take its own direction. Record all that is said.

– Read the script silently and then aloud. Take note of any feelings, emotions or energies which rise for you while doing so. Compare what rises for you now with what you felt when the script was being written.

The dialogue relationship which has been started with this wisdom figure continues, and may be added to at a later stage, or it may be extended in other relevant sections of the Journal. For example, a dialogue exercise may take us back to Intersections: Roads Taken and Not Taken; or it may take us back to the Life History Log to record memories which have been triggered. This initial dialogue, with our chosen wisdom figure, also leads us to dialogue with the other wisdom figures on our Steppingstones list. These Inner Wisdom Dialogues help us to live our lives at a progressively deeper level and to reach into the archetypal realm.

Now: The Open Moment

The Journal Workshop will end with the section, Now: The Open Moment. Participants in the Journal Workshop find themselves in a place between the past and the future. As people prepare to return to their homes and daily activity, after this *Sabbath time* apart, a new unit of time is beginning in their lives. Progoff calls this the Open Moment which is dawning before them. The participants are invited to:

– Sit in stillness and go back over the various entries in the Journal workbook.
– Feel the wholeness of the perspective of life which has been crystallizing.
– Be open to a further flow of feeling, thought and imagery, and the possibilities of the Open Moment of the future.

– Record the possibilities of the Open Moment in what-ever form they come, e.g. twilight imagery; a conscious recapitulation; a summary statement; a stream of thoughts; a prayer, etc.
 – Hold this written account or description in silence.
 – Draw the workshop experience to a close in peace and return to the activities of the outer world.

The workshop experience does not end here, and many Open Moments are waiting to unfold in the future. The experience continues and, as Progoff notes, "...the Intensive Journal process is our inner workshop, the place where we do the creative shaping of the artwork of our life".[5]

Summary

Taking our pen for a walk across the pages of a Journal is radical story-shaping. This exercise gives our core creative Self the space and freedom to express itself. Working with the *Intensive Journal* method aids the discovery of our psychic blueprint and our God-given individuality. Our *personal vocation*, or God-given name, is engraved in the exterior reality of our lives and it is written into our interior movements. The integrative format of Ira Progoff's *Intensive Journal* process brings the different strands of our life together. The dynamic of Feedback reveals our life-patterns and we grow in an ever-deepening awareness of the unique and God-given spirit which animates us.

Walking through the Steppingstones of our life brings the fresh air of consciousness. It softens and loosens the soil of our life so that our inner land can have its wedding and be fertile.

This walk through the Steppingstones of our life – the Steppingstones of both consolation and desolation – connects us with the Keystone or Cornerstone: with that underlying Reality which holds ultimate meaning for us and for the universe. This journey, in the belief that we are held by a greater Reality, leads us in an ever-deepening spiral toward the white stone with our God-given name and deepest identity. It leads to the ongoing birth of the Self.

NOTES

1 Ira Progoff, *At a Journal Workshop* (New York: Dialogue House, 1975) 64.
2 ibid 84.
3 Cf ibid 99/100.
4 Robert Frost, 'The Road Less Travelled' in *The Poetry of Robert Frost*, ed. Edward Connery Latham (London: Jonathan Cape, 1969). With the permission of the Estate of Robert Frost.
5 ibid 177.
6 ibid 297.

Chapter 10

Jungian Typology:
Discovering your Type

...when it comes to the inferior function...we have an open wound or at least an open door through which anything might enter.

Carl G. Jung, *Analytical Psychology*

Carl Jung distinguishes a number of functions in consciousness, some of which deal with data coming from the outside environment, and others which relate to contents below the threshold of consciousness itself.

Jungian typology describes how individuals relate with the environment and process their experiences. Human beings process experiences through perception and evaluation.

Perception and Evaluation

Reality may be perceived in two ways: (a) through the sensation function and (b) through the intuition function. We experience and perceive reality through the use of our five senses, i.e. sight, sound, smell, taste and touch. Our five senses tell us that something is. However, there is a "sixth sense" which also helps us to perceive reality and this is intuition. Intuition is instinctive knowing. It speaks the language of having a "hunch". It sees around corners. It knows what lies beyond the bend. It reads between the lines. Jung describes intuition as "a sort of perception which does not go exactly by the senses, but it goes via the unconscious..."[1]

What is perceived may then be evaluated in two ways:

(a) through the function of thinking and (b) through the function of feeling. While sensation tells us that a thing is, thinking tells us what that thing is. Thinking gives a scientific name or dictionary meaning to the thing. Feeling, on the other hand, tells us what the thing is worth to us. It informs us of the values of things, and it is not to be confused with emotion or sentiment.[2]

Dominant and Inferior Functions

The four main functions of thinking, feeling, intuition and sensation each approach reality with a different slant, and the four are needed to give a whole or complete picture. However, the four functions do not develop equally in the individual and each individual has a dominant or preferred function. This means that the individual approaches reality from a particular point of view and the opposite approach lies undeveloped in the unconscious. The dominant function may be helped by one or both of the remaining functions.

When thinking is the dominant function in an individual's consciousness then feeling is the undeveloped inferior function. Conversely, thinking is the inferior function when feeling is in the dominant position. In these two cases the perceptive functions of sensation and intuition are the helping energies, wavering on the border between the conscious and the unconscious. Depending on the individual, the two helping functions may be equally developed, or one may be more developed than the other, or in some cases both may be undeveloped.

If sensation is the dominant function then intuition will be the inferior one and vice versa. In these cases the evaluative energies of thinking and feeling are in the subsidiary or helping positions.

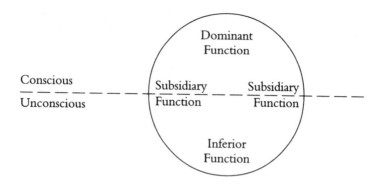

Inferior Function: An Open Wound

Jung described the inferior function as an open wound. Some might consider it unfortunate that the four functions are not equally developed in individuals, but Jung counts it a blessing. Firstly, he realizes that we can never reach perfection and that there will always be a flaw in the crystal. "Moreover," he states, "if we could differentiate the four functions equally we should only make them into consciously disposable functions. Then we would lose the most precious connection with the unconscious through the inferior function, which is invariably the weakest; only through our feebleness and incapacity are we linked up with the unconscious, with the lower world of the instincts and with our fellow beings."[3] Jung distinguishes between perfection and completion and he notes that our virtues only enable us to be independent since they take away our need of other people. It is in our inferiority or weakness that we are connected to humankind. The inferior function helps us to discover the unconscious and is a means of integrating the personality, a means of growth toward wholeness and completion.

The inferior function is related to the Shadow and is a "thorn in the flesh" which causes much of the problems and suffering in our lives. St Paul tells us he was given a thorn in the flesh to stop him from becoming too proud. He pleaded with the Lord three times, he declares, for this thorn to leave him but got the following answer: My grace is enough for you: my power is at its best in weakness (cf 2 Cor 12:7-10). The inferior function has been described as our God-connection. It is a wound in the psyche which allows unconscious life to flow into consciousness. It can open up new horizons and throw light on dark inner chambers.

Two Attitudes: Introversion and Extroversion

As well as the four typological functions of thinking, feeling, sensation and intuition, there are two attitudes which may work in conjunction with them. Jung used the words introversion and extroversion to describe the ebb and flow of psychic energy. When psychic energy ebbs toward the inner world of the individual it is introverted and when it flows outward to the exterior world it is extroverted. Each individual has an introverted and an extroverted side. However, individuals tend to have a preferred habit of channelling psychic energy either inwards or outwards.

Discovering your General Type

Jung warns about putting people into drawers with different labels and he stresses the uniqueness of each individual. His typology is merely a tool for classifying empirical information and it is a general aid on the pathway to self-discovery. Generally speaking, there are several possible combinations of the four functions and two attitudes. These combinations, however, simply hint at individual psychologies.

The Myers-Briggs Test
In the 1950s Isabel Myers and her mother K. Briggs designed a test known as the Myers-Briggs Type Indicator. This test is based on Jungian typology and is a tool for identifying

sixteen different psychological types. This test may be administered by a Jungian analyst or it is possible to attend workshops on the MBTI. Such workshops are still on offer in some Retreat Houses. People all over the world have used the MBTI to better their understanding of themselves and of others. Such understanding may improve communication in all spheres of life, both at home and in the workplace. The test may also prove helpful in choosing a career which is in tune with one's giftedness.

The test is based on a series of either-or questions which are intended to form patterns of an individual's preferences. For the test to be as accurate as possible, it is important to choose the preference which comes most spontaneously and naturally to you. The test is not foolproof and it is possible to choose a preference which is not your natural "fit". This may arise if you answer according to how you think you ought to be, or according to other people's expectations.

Sabbath Moments and Examination of Consciousness

Since it is possible to deceive ourselves when answering the questions on the Myers-Briggs Test, the most reliable way of discovering our typology is by observing our daily experiences. Ignatian spirituality encourages examinations of consciousness on a daily basis. These are brief *Sabbath times* for getting in touch with, and reflecting on, our real experience of the day.

The General Consciousness Examen is a gentle review of the whole day and the following steps may be helpful:

1. Thanksgiving
   God wants to incarnate in us. God is always coming into our lives, trying to break through into ego-consciousness. We thank God for constantly crossing the threshold of consciousness and, by doing so, express a desire to be actively receptive to God and to God's saving and reclaiming action.

2. Experience
   Ask for the grace to get in touch with your real
   experience of the day whether it is positive or negative.
   Accept this real experience. Awareness does not mean
   automatic acceptance. Do not judge it. Try not to
   deny it.

3. Response
   Let the ways in which you have been sensitive to
   God's presence rise up spontaneously to consciousness.
   Let the ways in which you missed God's presence
   also rise up spontaneously.

4. Pardon
   Ask God's pardon for missing any encounter; for not
   being centred; for any "blind spot" which led to
   another's pain.

5. Openness
   Invite God to grace your consciousness. Express a
   desire to be more open to the voice of God calling
   you by name in the depths of your being; the voice of
   God calling you into the wholeness of truth.

The Particular Examination of Consciousness punctuates
the whole day and is more focused and specific. These
punctuated *Sabbath times*, throughout the day, will sensitize
us to different modes of functioning.

Our inferior function tends to be the stumbling-block in
everyday living. If we belittle our inferior function as an
inadequate means of adapting to life, then we will tend to
disparage people who have this function as their dominant
one. Much of our misunderstandings, blunders, fears and
prejudices revolve around our inferior function.

Usually when people are asked to make a list of their
strong and weak points, the weak points come more easily
and outnumber the strong ones. This is so because we tend

to take our strong dominant characteristics for granted. Consequently, our inferior function, manifesting itself in our daily weaknesses, is a good indicator for our particular type. Our weaknesses show our strengths. Parts of the following checklist may be helpful for a particular examination of consciousness:

1. Do I tend to take everything literally?
   Do people tell me to be more imaginative?
   Have I been gullible in any way?
   Do I fail to read between the lines?
   Do I fail to hear what people do not say?
   Do I not see the wood for the trees? i.e. see detail but not the whole picture?

If the answer to these questions is "yes", then you are most probably a sensate type and your inferior intuition function is tripping you up!

2. Have I been criticised for poor punctuality?
   Do I ever forget about appointments?
   Am I considered a dreamer?
   Am I ever accused of being unrealistic?
   Do I tend to miss the obvious? i.e. see the wood but not the trees?

If the answer to these questions is "yes", then you are probably an intuitive type and your inferior sensation function is causing you trouble!

3. Do I get accused of being insensitive?
   Do I say inappropriate things in delicate or emotionally-charged situations?
   Do I tend to be cold and aloof?
   Do I tend to be rigidly moral – black and white when it comes to rules and regulations?

If the answer to these questions is "yes", then you are

probably a thinking type and your inferior feeling function is a stumbling-block!

4. Do I tend to be scatterbrained?
   Do I ever jump to false conclusions?
   Could my powers of analysis be better?
   Do I tend to have a secondhand philosophy?

If the answer to these questions is "yes", then you are probably a feeling type and your inferior thinking function is being problematic!

The particular and general consciousness examens are a means of effecting character transformation, and they are best approached in a spirit of gentleness, acceptance and compassion. It may be helpful to keep the following steps in mind:

1. While acknowledging your weaknesses and inferior function, begin by focusing on your giftedness and strength, in other words on your natural dominant function. Be grateful for such giftedness. Spend time on "fine tuning" this gift. This beginning time may stretch from days to weeks to months, and remains part of the other steps.

2. When you have spent time on accepting, appreciating and fine tuning your dominant function, then turn your attention to your two natural helping functions. Again be grateful for such giftedness and spend time developing these gifts.

3. Simply be open to the advent into consciousness of your fourth function which is your inferior one. Do not try to force the development of your inferior function. Usually the inferior function surfaces in mid-life, and, if allowed to develop in its own mysterious way, it brings new life and opens up new horizons.

Summary

This chapter is a brief and simplified introduction to Jungian typology which describes how individuals have a preferred way of functioning and of adapting to reality. We adapt to reality by perceiving and evaluating. Perception has two pathways: (a) through the five senses and (b) through the "sixth sense" of intuition. Evaluation, also, has two channels: a) through thinking and b) through feeling. When one of these pathways or channels is dominant, then its alternative "partner" is inferior.

Tests such as the Myers-Briggs Type Indicator may prove helpful in the discovery of our particular type. However, self-observation through a daily consciousness examen is probably the most reliable method of discovering our strengths and weaknesses, our dominant and inferior functions.

The inferior function is our stumbling-block in everyday living but it is also our God-connection. The inferior function is buried in the unconscious and is related to the Shadow which is the doorway to our individuality and deepest Self. It is instrumental in the process of integrating the conscious and unconscious aspects of personality and, if we allow it to develop to its own mysterious rhythm, it opens up new horizons and broadens our perspective. This opening up of new horizons helps to break down prejudices and better relationships between people who are "different". As a weakness or wound it is a doorway for the entry of new life, for the entry of God.

NOTES

1   Carl G. Jung, *Analytical Psychology: Its Theory and Practice* (London: Routledge/Ark, (1968) 1990) 14.
2   Cf ibid 13.
3   ibid 109.

Chapter 11

"Dream Catchers"

Much of the personal significance of symbolism is lost if you don't work out which is your dominant function, and which is your inferior. Dreams continuously refer to the functions that are atrophying in the unconscious: partial glimpses of facets of your personality which require attention.

Tom Chetwynd, *A Dictionary of Symbols*

Dreams play a central role in both the Old and New Testaments and, despite centuries of suspicion in the history of the Christian tradition, they are resurfacing, once again, to reveal their hidden treasures.

In native American mythology the story of the Dream Catcher is among the most beautiful and touching. It is part of this tradition to weave circular webs and place them above the cradles of the newly born. The purpose of the woven web is to catch and filter dreams, allowing only the good ones to flow through the open circle. This chapter is a brief exploration of the significance of dreams and of how we, ourselves, can be "Dream Catchers". Let's begin by meeting some Biblical ones.

Biblical Dream Catchers

The Book of Job tells us that, "God speaks in one way, and in two, though people do not perceive it. In a dream, in a vision of the night, when deep sleep falls on mortals, while they slumber on their beds..." (Job 33:14,15). Dream language is God's song in the darkness of the night (cf Ps 42:8); it is the music of the night which God provides for the beloved one during sleep (cf Ps 127:2). In chapter 2 we met

Jacob who had a transformative encounter with God and was called by the new name of "Israel". His dream of a ladder stretching from heaven to earth is probably the most striking dream in the whole Bible:

> Jacob left Beer-sheba and went toward Haran. He came to a certain place and stayed there for the night, because the sun had set. Taking one of the stones of the place, he put it under his head and lay down in that place. And he dreamed that there was a ladder set up on the earth, the top of it reaching to heaven; and the angels of God were ascending and descending on it. And the Lord stood beside him and said, "I am the Lord, the God of Abraham your father and the God of Isaac; the land on which you lie I will give to you and to your offspring; and your offspring shall be like the dust of the earth, and you shall spread abroad to the west and to the east and to the north and to the south; and all the families of the earth shall be blessed in you and in your offspring. Know that I am with you and will keep you wherever you go, and will bring you back to this land; for I will not leave you until I have done what I have promised you." Then Jacob woke from his sleep and said, "Surely the Lord is in this place – and I did not know it!" And he was afraid, and said, "How awesome is this place! This is none other than the house of God, and this is the gate of heaven." (Gen 28:10-17)

At this point on Jacob's journey a split has taken place between him and his brother Esau, and Jacob is faced with alienation and exile. In his alienated state Jacob is graced with a dream of union: union between heaven and earth; matter and spirit; the human and divine; time and eternity; the four directions of the land. The dream vision of Jacob's offspring, spreading to the four corners of the earth – North, South, East and West – echoes Abraham's earlier vision and his covenant with Yahweh. From a Jungian perspective, the dream imagery represents the ego-Self axis, and Jacob's split with Esau represents the conflict between the ego and the shadow. In this dream, Jacob is graced with a foretaste of the mystical marriage to come.

To mark his experience in dream time and dream space, Jacob, on awakening, took the stone which he had placed under his head as a pillow and he set it up as a pillar, naming it Bethel, i.e. House of God (cf Gen 28:18-22). Again we come across the image of stone. Here it may symbolize that aspect of Jacob which endures, i.e. his divine Centre, his deepest and truest Self. By "catching" his dream in the symbol of stone, Jacob's experience and story has endured down to the present day.

The best known dreamer and dream interpreter in the Old Testament is Joseph with his long-sleeved or multi-coloured dream-robe.[1] Joseph was Israel's (Jacob's) favourite son, and Israel bestowed on him a special, distinctive robe. This distinctive robe represents the Self, but the young Joseph identifies the Self with his ego and incurs the dangers of ego-inflation. His tell-tale activity (cf Gen 37:2), and the recounting of his dreams, which place him in a position of dominance over his brothers, add to their feelings of jealousy and hatred. His ego-inflation invites hostility and he is stripped of his distinctive robe and sold as a slave into Egypt.

While in Egypt Joseph used his graced God-connection to interpret dreams (cf Gen 40ff). All the dreams which were brought to his awareness presented a tension between pairs of opposites. This symbolizes Joseph's own need to integrate the opposites within himself, so that he can de-velop a conscious relationship with the Self rather than an ego-identification with it. By doing so he preserves life (cf Gen 45:5). Egypt, the place of bondage, becomes the place of nourishment and relief.

Later, in New Testament times, Egypt becomes a place of refuge for another dreamer called Joseph: the foster father of the Messiah. Warned by a dream, he, Mary and Jesus flee into Egypt to escape the binding threat of Herod (cf Mt 2:13). The Magi, too, are warned in a dream about the dangers of Herod and they leave for their own country by another road (cf Mt 2:12). Herod may represent an insecure ego which cannot tolerate and is threatened by any new psychic principle. Joseph, on the other hand, may represent a healthy, flexible ego which can endure the shock of realizing there is a greater parent, the shock of discovering it is not master in its own household (cf Mt 1:18-20; Lk 2:49). If we are to reach our own country – our own interior and spacious land – we cannot remain on Herod's narrow road.

When Herod and his threat to the Christ-child dies, Joseph is again graced with a dream and is called back to the land of Israel. However, danger still surrounds Herod's successor, and Joseph receives another dream-warning about returning to the land of Judea. Instead he goes to the district of Galilee: an area held in disdain by the "pure Jews" of Judea; an area of rolling hills and deep inland sea; an area of contrast and home-coming. It was in this place that Jesus grew and became strong, filled with wisdom; and the favour of God was upon him (Lk 2:40).

As an adult, Jesus comes face to face with hostile external authority and, once again, his very life is in danger. Despite the risk and danger he does not compromise the truth of his being. This truth is revealed to Pilate's wife in a dream and she sends word to Pilate as he sits on the judgement seat: "Have nothing to do with that innocent man, for today I have suffered a great deal because of a dream about him."(Mt 27:19) However, Pilate does not have the courage to listen to his feminine soul and he gives way to the collective, to the demands of the bloodthirsty mob. Paradoxically, though, Jesus' crucifixion and woundedness lead to new life. The Spirit pours through his open wounds. His wounds are the channel for the energizing, resurrecting Spirit; for the Spirit of both disturbing and comforting truth who is also promised to us in our woundedness and brokenness.

On the day of Pentecost, the broken Peter, the failed Peter, the humbled Peter is filled with the life and energy of the Spirit. He fearlessly addresses the crowds in Jerusalem and quotes the prophet Joel, encouraging his listeners to dream dreams:

> In the last days – the Lord declares –
> I shall pour out my Spirit on all humanity.
> Your sons and daughters shall prophesy,
> your young people shall see visions,
> your old people dream dreams...
> (Acts 2:17 JB trans.; Joel 2:28,29)

The Significance of Dreams

When we enter dream space we encounter soul in a special way. The soul is the interface of time and eternity. At the still point of the soul's dynamic turning all opposites meet. Soul is the place of the substantial Word. It is the power-house which generates symbol, myth and meaning.

Dreams are Godspeak. They are channels of divine revelation. During sleep the barriers which are erected by the ego are let down, and in our dreams we are carried by the flow of symbolic imagery welling up from the unconscious and our deepest Centre. We are carried on eagles' wings to the heights and depths of our being and to God's very own Self (cf Ex 19:4). Here we brush against the creative heart of God and, consequently, dreams are associated with the creative impulse and inspiration of artists, innovators and inventors. Through our dreams God calls us into new creations. Through our dream symbols God calls us into the deepening spiral of becoming – the spiral of becoming our deepest and truest Self, grounded in body, soul and spirit. The creative finger of God writes a pattern through our dream sequences and Jung called this pattern-making the process of individuation. Dreams are a driving force on the

135

pathway to individuation and the discovery of our God-given individuality.

Dream symbols are part of the natural fabric which builds a bridge between the ego (island) and the unconscious (large hinterland). As Tom Chetwynd notes, much of the personal significance of symbolism is lost if we do not discover which is our conscious dominant function and which is our inferior function latent in the unconscious.[2] In our dreams we encounter facets of our personality which need attention for our growth toward wholeness and holiness. The inferior function has been described as a wound or an open door. Through dream-wounding the life and energy of the Spirit can flow into consciousness; the wind of God can sweep over the dark face of the deep and bring the light of awareness (cf Gen 1:2). Through dream-wounding we are healed and made whole.

Dream Catching

Everybody dreams. Not everybody "catches" every dream. Sometimes dreams disappear from the edges of consciousness like wisps of smoke. We reach out to touch the experience but it has gone. It has slipped the net of consciousness and floated back into the deep from whence it came.

The following are some suggestions which may help to strengthen our net of consciousness and to encourage the dream experience to linger with us:

1. Get in touch with your desire around dream recall. Do you really want to remember your dreams? Sometimes we meet the shadow-side of ourselves in our dreams and this can be a very painful experience. However, the Shadow is the doorway to our deepest Centre. Do you want to go through the pain of awareness so that you can discover your God-given individuality?

2. If you really want to remember your dreams, a ritual such as the following may be helpful before retiring to bed:

— Turn off the main lights and light a candle. As you light the candle say a prayer such as the following: "As I light this candle may it remind me of the divine spark at the heart of my being." Watch the dancing flame dispel the darkness around it and say part of Psalm 23 or Isaiah 43:1,2:

> Even though I walk through the darkest valley,
> > I fear no evil;
> for you (my God) are with me;
> > your rod and your staff –
> > they comfort me (Ps 23:4).

> Do not fear, for I have redeemed you;
> > I have called you by name,
> > > you are mine.
> When you pass through the
> > waters, I will be with you... (Is 43:1,2a)

— Invite the wind of God to sweep over the waters of your unconscious as you sleep. Express your desire for God to speak to you in dream imagery and symbols.

— Place a dream journal or a tape recorder beside your bed so that if you awake during the night you can quickly note any images or words which will help dream recall. For a dream journal, it is best to use a file which can take single sheets of A4 paper. Using this format means that additional work on any dream can be added easily. If you are attracted to Progoff's *Intensive Journal* method, there is a Dream Log section and a Dream Enlargement section.

— Drift into the darkness of sleep with an attitude of openness to, and anticipation of, God's communication.

3. When possible write your dream text immediately on remembering your dream. Do not trust your memory for a later time. The dream or dream fragments might slip the net

of consciousness and return to the obscurity of the deep. The following guidelines may be helpful when creating your dream text:

– Write the dream in the present rather than the past tense. Use of the past tense in creating a dream text tends to distance the experience of the dream. Use of the present tense, on the other hand, helps us to reconnect with the dream experience.

– Using the present tense, gather your dream experience around the following pointers:

• Describe the location in the dream. Are there any striking features in this location?
• What time is it? Is it light or dark?
• Describe the people in the dream and their activity.
• Are there any other figures present, e.g. supernatural or abstract?
• Describe any other creatures which may be in the dream, e.g. animals, insects, birds...
• What are the feelings in the dream? What is the overall mood?
• Gathering your information around the above pointers, write your dream text following the simple structure of any story-line:
  Opening scene
  Development of plot
  Conclusion

The plot in dreams often develops with a bizarre twist and the conclusion of a dream may be solution or crisis. If your dream ends in a crisis or wakes you up, it means something has to be resolved in waking life.

• Give the dream text a title and date it.

4. Having created your dream text in prose, you might like to express the dream experience in another form. The following are some possibilities:

– Write a poem, "capturing" the dream experience in a pattern of words and rhythm.

– Do a painting, "capturing" the experience of the dream in patterns of line and colour.

– Using clay, get in touch with the dream experience and let your unconscious mould a shape.

– Let your body draw its own pattern in space through movement and dance. Perhaps this movement could be captured on video.

Understanding Dream Language

Dream language is multifaceted and holds many layers of meaning. Consequently, as Jung points out, it is impossible to formulate a general theory of dreams. The following formulation is the nearest that Jung could get to a theory about their structure and function: "Dreams are the natural reaction of the self-regulating psychic system."[3] This means that dreams have a compensatory relationship with consciousness and they function to bring the whole psyche into balance. They express the unconscious and an alternative point of view, often correcting our conscious judgements and attitudes. They reveal the interior dynamics of the individual, and the images in dreams represent various parts of the individual's personality. Jung warns about applying theories in the interpretation of another person's dreams. The starting point is the context of the dreamer's life and the dreamer's feelings toward the dream images. Ultimately, the dreamer is the only authority on the meaning of his or her dream, but the assistance of another person in looking at the dream adds clarity and objectivity.

Jung, however, distinguishes between two kinds of dreams. One kind of dream belongs to the personal level and is formed of personal material. To understand the language of these dreams, they must be placed, as already stated, in the context of the dreamer's life and the individual's associations with the dream images need to be explored. This kind of dream speaks a personal language. The second kind of dream is a rather rare experience. This kind belongs to the collective level and speaks a universal language. It has a mythological structure and holds collective meaning. To understand the language of these "big" dreams, a knowledge of universal mythology, legends and fairy tales is necessary. Since this kind of dream speaks a universal language it is possible to grasp its meaning without detailed knowledge of and reference to the individual dreamer.

Whether our dreams are on the personal level or on the collective level they speak the language of symbol. When it comes to the language of symbols most of us hover on the borderline between being literate and illiterate. To understand our dreams we need to learn a new language which is nonrational, ambiguous, nuanced and pregnant with meaning.

When you have written your dream text, and perhaps expressed the dream experience in other ways, the following pointers may be helpful in understanding the language of your dream:

Contextualize the dream; i.e. write an account of what is currently happening in your waking life. Then,

(a) Check for a literal meaning; i.e. is your dream a literal exposition of external world events and meaning? Does it contain objective truth? Is it a warning? Is it a reminder?

(b) Having checked for any literal meaning, then examine the dream as a metaphorical statement of your relationships and of your feelings.

(c) Check for any intra-psychic meaning; i.e. is the dream a symbolic exposition of relationships within yourself; a symbolic exposition of your own interior dynamics?

The following questions may help you to check for the above levels of meaning:

— Do you know any of the characters in your dream from

waking life? If yes, describe your relationship. Is the dream saying anything about this relationship in waking life?

What do you associate with this person or persons?

Does the person or persons have any particular striking feature or characteristic in the dream? Does this outstanding feature or characteristic represent some part of you?

– Are there characters in the dream not known to you in waking life? To which sex do these characters belong? Unknown characters with the same sex as the dreamer may represent the dreamer's shadow-side, while unknown characters of the opposite sex may represent the anima or animus.

– Do any other images or features in the dream represent a part of you? For example, if there is a house in your dream does its appearance and condition say something about some aspect of your personality?

– Make note of the spontaneous associations you have with every image in the dream. Your associations may include a word, a feeling, a memory, an idea, a person, etc.; i.e. whatever rises up spontaneously in association with the image.

– As you linger with the associations which have arisen, see if any one "clicks" or resonates deeply with you. When something does "click" you have tapped into a deep spring of energy. Let this energy flow.

– Third party information about family events and experiences may also prove helpful on occasions. For example, there may be some significant experience from childhood which you cannot recall, such as the kind of birth you had; an early illness, perhaps, or some traumatic event.

– Did your dream have a mythical or fairy tale quality about it? Check your dream for any archetypes. This may be done by a procedure which Jung called amplification. It simply means seeking parallels in myths and fairy tales and ancient religious traditions. However, in practice it could mean extensive research. This is where the training and expertise of a Jungian therapist could be very helpful.

Dream On: Active Imagination

Basically there are three ways of dreaming: a) night-dreaming which occurs in the unconscious realm of sleep; b) daydreaming which occurs during waking hours, but when the ego exerts little, if no control, and is carried passively along by fantasies; c) active imagination which is another kind of waking dream, but when the ego is consciously involved and focused. All of these dreaming styles can tell us very interesting things about ourselves.

Active imagination is particularly helpful as it enables us to consciously interact with, and to consciously explore, our night-dream images and symbols. However, it is a technique which needs to be used with some caution. There is an element of danger since our imagination could "run away with us" and we could lose touch with the reality about us in waking life. Again this is where a therapist, or some other skilled person with whom we can talk, could prove very helpful.

Active imagination involves a conscious ego-participation in an imaginative experience which is purposeful creation. It is a powerful technique which invites the unconscious and the conscious to meet, to play, to dialogue and, through their interaction, to give birth to a wisdom from the deep.

— As in dream work, it is important to invite the unconscious to speak to you through active imagination.
— It is also important to record the experience by using some of the different methods already outlined for the recording of dreams. When writing a prose text for this kind of work, however, it is helpful to use the format of a dialogue as in the text of a play.
— Choose some *Sabbath time* when you will not be interrupted.
— Active imagination begins by concentrating on a starting point. This starting point may be a dream image or a dream figure; or it may be a picture or painting from waking life.

– Concentrate on the image until the image begins to move and develop.

– Do not let your conscious reason interfere with this movement and development. Do not analyse the experience while it is happening. Let the image unfold and observe its spontaneous changes.

– Become an active observer, i.e. dialogue and interact with the image or figure. Let your feelings and emotions get involved.

– This technique may also be helpful for getting in touch with our feelings, emotions and moods. We can ask the unconscious to personify our feelings etc. so that we can dialogue with them and grow in awareness, understanding and moral responsibility.

Robert A. Johnson points out that,

> When Active Imagination is done correctly, it pulls the different parts of you together that have been fragmented or in conflict... It sets one off on a path toward wholeness, toward an awareness of one's larger totality, simply because one has learned to enter into communication with the inner self.[4]

Dream On: Imaginative Contemplation

In the *Spiritual Exercises*, St Ignatius presents a form of prayer known as imaginative contemplation. This form of prayer existed in the Christian tradition before Ignatius, but he tailored it to suit his purposes in the Exercises. It is a form of prayer which may be compared to active imagination. David Londsdale S.J. describes it thus:

> While this kind of contemplation engages the whole person with the varied capacities and powers that belong to the human person, it also gives a special

143

place to imagination and the different levels of feeling and commitment which can be touched and moved through the imagination.[5]

Imaginative contemplation involves focusing on a scene from the gospels and entering into that scene with the gift of imagination. As the word of God becomes alive and active, it draws the individual into the picture and begins to speak to the heart.

— Choose your *Sabbath time* and a place where you will not be disturbed.
— Choose a scene from the gospels.
— Invite God to speak to you in this time of prayer and imaginative contemplation.
— Read the scripture passage slowly – more than once if necessary.
— Put your Bible aside and focus on the scene.
— Let the characters and images move and develop spontaneously. Use all of your senses:
  • observe what is happening;
  • listen to the sounds and voices;
  • smell any scents in the air;
  • taste any food or drink or even the atmosphere;
  • reach out and touch the ground or the nearest thing or person to you.

— Take part in the scene. Interact with the other characters and with Jesus. Ask questions. Wait for a response. Get involved.
— At the end of the story take some time to dialogue with Jesus or another main character about what has happened. Say how the experience has been for you.
— When you are ready, say good-bye and leave the place.
— Bring your time of contemplation to an end by saying a prayer such as the Our Father.
— Go to another place and reflect for a few moments on the whole experience. In a prayer journal, jot down any insights, feelings or significant movements.

Imaginative contemplation connects us with cosmic, archetypal figures and forces, and we are drawn into the battleground of our own souls. Here we meet ourselves in biblical characters and images. Here we encounter Christ: our deepest and truest Self; the source and secret of our unity and meaning in life.

Summary

Dreaming is a universal experience and it plays a central role in both the Old and New Testaments. In contrast to the modern, rationalistic mind of the West, biblical characters were open to the presence of God, breaking into consciousness, through the medium of dreams and visions. Despite centuries of suspicion in the Christian tradition and a rationalistic outlook, dreams are being reclaimed as Godspeak.

Dreams are channels of divine revelation. They wound our consciousness with the realization that there is a greater Centre beyond the ego. They wound our hearts with a desire for unity and integration. They call us into the depths of our God-given individuality, inviting us to look at facets of our personality which require attention for our growth toward wholeness and holiness.

We are called to be dream catchers. We have been gifted by God with the creative power of imagination. We are invited to enter the language of symbol and to uncover its many layers of meaning. We are invited to trace it to the very core of our being.

We are called to be dream catchers for the Kingdom: for the Kingdom within and the Kingdom without. God invites us to leave familiar shores and to take a step out into the deep. God asks us to tread softly and with growing awareness, because She has spread Her dreams under our feet!

Had I the heaven's embroidered cloths,
Enwrought with golden and silver light,
The blue and the dim and the dark cloths
Of night and light and the half-light,
I would spread the cloths under your feet:
But I, being poor, have only my dreams;
I have spread my dreams under your feet;
Tread softly because you tread on my dreams.

W.B. Yeats, 'He Wishes for the Cloths of Heaven'

NOTES

1 The traditional Hebrew rendering is "*a robe with long sleeves*". The Greek version says, "*a coat of many colours*".

2 Cf Tom Chetwynd, *A Dictionary of Symbols* (London: Paladin/Collins, 1982) 161.

3 Carl G. Jung, *Analytical Psychology*, 124.

4 Robert A. Johnson, *Inner Work,* 141/142.

5 David Lonsdale S.J., *Eyes to See, Ears to Hear* (London: Darton, Longman & Todd, 1990) 89.

6 W.B. Yeats, 'He Wishes for the Cloths of Heaven' in *The Collected Poems of W.B. Yeats* (London: Macmillan/Picador, (1933) 1990) 81. By the permission of A.P. Watt Ltd on behalf of Michael Yeats.

Chapter 12

Lectio Divina:
Divine Reading

Meditative reading is a dwelling on the text,
drilling and spiralling, so to speak, until the
treasure of life transforming meanings spring up.
Adrian van Kaam, *The Woman at the Well*

Lectio divina is an ancient method of prayer and Scripture-reading which dates back to the early centuries of Christianity. Two types of *lectio* may be distinguished in the history of theological reflection. One is monastic *lectio* (more accurately called community *lectio*) which was the customary method until scholastic *lectio* became increasingly dominant from the eighth century onward. Scholastic *lectio* strove for science and knowledge through *quaestio* and *disputatio* i.e. through questioning and argument or debate. In contrast, monastic *lectio* went beyond intellectual activity, taking the direction of *meditatio* and *oratio*. It sought to engage the whole person, desiring wisdom rather than knowledge. It saw informative reading as providing a solid foundation, but it asked the further question, "What does this text mean for me and for my life situation?" It is this type of holistic and formative reading which is referred to as *lectio divina*.

The following diagram helps to illustrate the dynamic of this divine or sacred reading. Some writers include *contemplatio* as a fourth step and I have chosen to do so even though it is not considered proper to the tradition by some. It is important to remember that ideally these steps happen simultaneously and in a deepening spiralling movement, rather than separately.

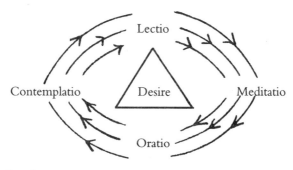

1. *Lectio*

The first step, *lectio*, requires attentive study of the text of Scripture and a reverence for the text as it is. Attentive study might include exegetical clarification but it is *more than* intellectual activity; it is a work of the *heart* and, therefore, of the whole personality.

In ancient times and in the Middle Ages, the practice of reading differed considerably from what we are accustomed to today. The monks of early Christianity used as many of the senses as possible. They read not only with their eyes but with their lips, savouring the shape and texture of the words and hearing their vibrations. The pages were alive with shapes and voices. This more active style of reading led to a "whole" memorization, since it involved the visual memory of the eyes; the oral, muscular memory of the lips forming the words; and the aural memory of the ears recording the sounds. The whole person was steeped in the words of Scripture until the exterior murmuring of the lips became an interior murmuring of the heart.

2. *Meditatio*

Lectio and *meditatio* cannot really be separated, since *meditatio* is the interiorization of the reading process. The word *ruminatio* is used to describe *lectio-meditatio* whereby the words of Scripture are ruminated on in the *palatum cordis*, the palate of the heart, and their juices allowed to trickle on the heart's interior lips. Jean Leclercq describes *meditatio* as follows:

To meditate is to attach oneself closely to the sentence being recited and weigh all its words in order to sound the depths of their full meaning. It means assimilating the content of a text by means of a kind of mastication which releases its full flavour.[1]

When the text reveals a hidden treasure or truth for the individual, he or she lingers with it, relishing its flavour and fragrance. This is similar to an incubation period which fosters creativity and provides space for spontaneous associations to develop. The text comes alive and the individual begins to associate fragments of the text with the bits and pieces of his or her every day life. The individual realises that he or she experienced a similar situation; thought a similar thought, perhaps; felt a similar feeling; met similar characters on the journey through life. Jean Leclercq refers to this as the phenomenon of reminiscence, whereby words act like hooks attracting fragments of our experience, and verbal echoes excite the memory.[2]

3. Oratio

Oratio, or prayer, is a rather deceptive word for those of us living in the twentieth century, since the whole process would be considered prayer by us. In the context of *lectio divina*, *oratio* is basically a prayer of desire and petition.

Lectio and *meditatio* have been described as a half-way house on the individual's journey to God. One may opt to go no further, feeling satisfied with the ground covered, or feeling afraid of losing control. Others, however, may be urged on by a feeling of dissatisfaction and the feeling of an unfinished journey. These feelings may be accompanied by a sense of helplessness, and a humble acknowledgement that one cannot proceed without assistance from a Greater Power, without the special help of God.

Oratio, then, may take the form of thanksgiving; i.e. the utterance of a grateful heart for being brought so far on the journey, despite one's faults, failings and limitations. The *oratio* may rise from a very lonely space; from a deep sense of alienation, perhaps, because of one's sinfulness and fragmentation. It is a place of radical poverty and dependence. But at the heart of the *oratio* is the prayer of desire, the longing to see the face of God, the thirsting for ecstatic union:

> O God, you are my God, I seek you,
> > my soul thirsts for you;
> > my flesh faints for you... (Ps 63,1).

> Hear, O Lord, when I cry aloud,
> be gracious to me and answer me!
> "Come," my heart says, "seek his face!"
> Your face, Lord, do I seek.
> Do not hide your face from me (Ps 27,7-9).

> ...Lord, show us the Father, and we will be satisfied (Jn 14:8).

> O living flame of love
> That tenderly wounds my soul
> In its deepest centre!...
> ....if it be your will:
> Tear through the veil of this sweet encounter![3]

The symbol of the veil may be seen in two lights. It may be seen as a block or resistance to the working of the Spirit, and in the *oratio* we need to beg for God's help in removing any obstacles or attachments which impede our openness to the Spirit of God. On the other hand, the veil which hides the face and fullness of God is necessary to preserve mystery. "Without the veil," Linda Schierse Leonard explains, "the mystery is lost, and with it the possibility for the sacred marriage... For the soul is lost when mystery is taken away... Only if the veil is there can it be lifted. Only then can we experience the divine ecstasy described by the poet Rumi:

This is love: to fly toward a secret sky,
to cause a hundred veils to fall each moment.
First to let go of life.
Finally, to take a step without feet.[4]

4. Contemplatio

In the practice of *lectio divina, contemplatio* is pure gift, and the fleeting fulfilment of the heart's desire. The individual takes a step without feet and lets go into God. It is when God lifts the veil and takes over the individual's prayer. The Infinite breaks into consciousness: the substantial or interior Word rises up to enlighten the mind and to inflame the heart:

> I confess to you I have many times received the visits of the Word. I could not perceive the exact moment of his arrival. He did not enter by the senses, but whence did he come? Perhaps he did not enter at all, for he who enters comes from without. But I found him closer to me than I am to myself... He moves and warms and wounds my heart, hard and stony and sick though it be.[5]

In the contemplative moment, the individual catches a glimpse of his or her deepest Self hidden in the Eternal Logos and Eros. It is important to point out that the contemplative moment is not reserved for an elite. Remember that God wants to incarnate in you. It is vital to recall this desire, and not to let your own desire for union with self, others and God get smothered. Spending some *Sabbath time* with *lectio divina* may be one way of giving this desire space to delve and deepen.

Practical Suggestions for Sabbath-time Reading

– Choose a time and place where you will not be disturbed for at least fifteen minutes.

- Ideally, this time is taken on a daily basis.
- Try to keep to this time and place so that your whole personality, body-soul-spirit, will come to anticipate it and look forward to it.
- Don't rush into this sacred space. Stop for a few seconds and remember that you are about to enter holy ground.
- Choose the forthcoming Sunday gospel from the liturgical cycle.
- Stay with this text for the whole week. Clarify any points of information at the beginning and then let the text come alive for you.
- Use as many of your senses as possible when reading and meditating on the text.
- Use the language and imagery of the text during your prayer-time and, if you feel comfortable enough, use the language and imagery in conversation outside of *Sabbath time*.
- Finding a soul mate with whom you can share your experience may be helpful and enlightening.
- Writing about your experiences in a journal may also be helpful, and it may draw your awareness to unfolding patterns.

A Selection of Texts

The Feast of Christ the King
Cycle A

> Jesus said to his disciples: "When the Son of Man comes in his glory, escorted by all the angels, then he will take his seat on his throne of glory. All the nations will be assembled before him and he will separate people one from another as the shepherd separates sheep from goats. He will place the sheep on his right hand and the goats on his left. Then the King will say to those on his right hand, 'Come, you whom my Father has blessed, take for your heritage the kingdom prepared for you since the foundation

of the world. For I was hungry and you gave me food; I was thirsty and you gave me drink; I was a stranger and you made me welcome; naked and you clothed me, sick and you visited me, in prison and you came to see me.' Then the virtuous will say to him in reply, 'Lord, when did we see you hungry and feed you; or thirsty and give you drink? When did we see you a stranger and make you welcome; naked and clothed you; sick or in prison and go to see you?' And the King will answer, 'I tell you solemnly, in so far as you did this to one of the least of these brothers of mine, you did it to me.' Next he will say to those on his left hand, 'Go away from me, with your curse upon you, to the eternal fire prepared for the devil and his angels. For I was hungry and you never gave me food; I was thirsty and you never gave me anything to drink; I was a stranger and you never made me welcome, naked and you never clothed me, sick and in prison and you never visited me.' Then it will be their turn to ask, 'Lord, when did we see you hungry or thirsty, a stranger or naked, sick or in prison, and did not come to your help?' Then he will answer, 'I tell you solemnly, in so far as you neglected to do this to one of the least of these, you neglected to do it to me.' And they will go away to eternal punishment, and the virtuous to eternal life" (Mt 25:31-46; ST PAUL Sunday Missal 1996).

– Read the passage slowly and, preferably, out loud, repeating it several times.
– Stay and linger with any word, or phrase, or image which strikes you.
– Are you aware of any feelings, emotions or memories being triggered by your meditative reading?
  • an experience of being hungry or thirsty, perhaps?
  • maybe an embarrassing moment of feeling naked and vulnerable?

- a feeling of being trapped or imprisoned?
- the experience of being a stranger welcomed or rejected?
- a memory of being sick?

– Who were the people you encountered in these experiences? Were they helpful or unhelpful?

– How did you help yourself?

– Have you any memories of people coming to you for help? Asking for a favour, perhaps, or in need of alms? How did you respond?

– Pray in gratitude for the memories, feelings and emotions which have graced your awareness. Perhaps there is a need to pray for the healing of some hurt or injury. Maybe it is necessary to ask for the grace to forgive somebody who has overlooked you or neglected you. Ask forgiveness for your own faults and failings; for the times when you failed to reach out to those in need. Get in touch with God's desire to incarnate in you, and your desire for union with self, others and God. Implore God's help to fulfil this desire.

– Ask yourself if you are projecting your own despised shadow-side onto other people. Call yourself a "goat" if you think the beggar, the prisoner, the naked are not in yourself! Call yourself a "goat" if you think you are not in need of the alms of your own kindness because you are punishing yourself... and very likely the people with whom you live!

– Let God lead you through your shadow-side to your deepest Self, to the Kingdom within which will enable you to live a fuller life in the Kingdom without.

Cycle B

"Are you the king of the Jews?" Pilate asked. Jesus replied, "Do you ask this of your own accord, or have others spoken to you about me?" Pilate answered, "Am I a Jew? It is your own people and the chief priests who have handed you over to me: what have you done?" Jesus replied, "Mine is not a kingdom of this world; if my kingdom were of this world, my men would have fought to prevent my being surrendered to the Jews. But my kingdom is not of this kind." "So you are a king then?" said Pilate. "It is you who say it", answered Jesus. "Yes, I am a king. I was born for this, I came into the world for this: to bear witness to the truth; and all who are on the side of truth listen to my voice" (Jn 18:33-37; ST PAUL Sunday Missal 1997).

- Have you ever felt you were on trial or being tested?
- Have people ever challenged or questioned your identity?
- Have you ever struggled with your own identity?
- Who is Jesus for you?
- What is the truth of your being?
- Pray for the desire to listen to his voice, the inner voice of truth at the core of your being. Listen to your unconscious identity which, through the voices of the Persona, Shadow, Anima and Animus, tries to tear the veil of deafness; tries to break through our efforts at ignoring the truth.

Cycle C

The people stayed there watching Jesus. As for the leaders, they jeered at him. "He saved others," they said, "let him save himself if he is the Christ of God, the Chosen One." The soldiers mocked him too, and when they approached to offer him vinegar they said, "If you are the king of the Jews, save yourself." Above him was an inscription: "This is the King of the Jews."

One of the criminals hanging there abused him. "Are you not the Christ?" he said. "Save yourself and us as well." But the other spoke up and rebuked him. "Have you no fear of God at all?" he said. "You got the same sentence as he did, but in our case we deserved it: we are paying for what we did. But this man has done nothing wrong. Jesus," he said, "remember me when you come into your kingdom." "Indeed, I promise you," he replied, "today you will be with me in paradise" (Lk 23:35-43; ST PAUL Sunday Missal 1998).

– Have you ever had the experience of being watched or scrutinized? Do you stand watch over other people? Do you stand watch over yourself, scrutinizing and judging?
– Have you memories of being jeered at or mocked by others? Do you ever hear a voice within yourself, saying, "You are no good"; "You are a failure"; "Who do you think you are?"? What do you say about other people?
– Do you ever try to deny your humanity with its limitations? Do you accept death as a reality – symbolic and actual?
– Do you believe Jesus' words, "Indeed I promise you, today you will be with me in paradise"?
– Pray to be faithful to the humanity entrusted to you, and to the destiny implicit in it. Pray for the grace to be able to hold the crucifying opposites, so that you might live a fuller life.

Invite Everyone you can find to the Wedding
– Read Matthew 22:1-14
– Who do you identify with in this story?
  • Is it the King who has been snubbed?
  • Is it the recipients of the wedding invitations who are too busy with ego-ideals, perhaps; too busy "making a living" instead of living; reluctant to go, perhaps, because a wedding gift would cost too much; or simply too arrogant to recognize their need of the King?
  • Or is it the second lot of guests "bad and good alike"?
  • Or is it the "friend" who arrives without a wedding garment and is "out of place"?

Linda Schierse Leonard records a dream with a similar theme. She states:

> One man, in the beginning of his analysis, dreamed that he had been invited to the royal wedding of the king and queen. The royal couple was there and all the attendants were richly appointed. But when he looked down at his clothes he saw he was wearing old jeans and felt out of place. Upon awakening, he realized that he was not prepared for the divine wedding, and had a lot of work to do on himself before he could attend this sacred event.[6]

Our deepest Self, symbolized by the King in the scripture passage, will try to draw our attention to the fact that we are still bound in some way, that we still need to face the darkness and go through the suffering of the *nigredo* – even if that means "weeping and grinding of teeth". The call to the royal, divine wedding is a dynamic process. If we want to be at the wedding, we cannot choose to bypass the process. Therefore:

Stay Awake!

> "Be on your guard, stay awake, because you never know when the time will come. It is like a man travelling abroad: he has gone from home, and left his servants in charge, each with his own task; and he has told the doorkeeper to stay awake. So stay awake, because you do not know when the master of the house is coming: evening, midnight, cockcrow, dawn; if he comes unexpectedly, he must not find you asleep. And what I say to you I say to all: Stay awake!" (Mk 13:33-37; ST PAUL Sunday Missal 1997, First Sunday Of Advent).

The doorkeeper of the soul must stay awake, attentive to the movements in different shades and light: attentive to the movements in the dimness of eventide, in the deep darkness of midnight, in the breaking light of cockcrow, in the glorious colour of the dawn. If the owner arrives unexpectedly, the owner must be met with enthusiasm.

The word enthusiasm comes from *en theos* which means "engodded". If we stay awake to the movements of the Word and meet the Word with enthusiasm, whether in darkness or in light, then our reading will truly be divine.

Summary

When we enter into *lectio divina*, we allow the open-ended mystery of the text to speak to the open-ended mystery of our being. *Lectio divina* is putting unique skin on an ancient sacred story. There are many layers to this skin which the meditative rhythm of *lectio divina* peels back to reveal the text's deep core and the individual's deepest Centre. Approaching the core and centre implies that the Christ-message in the text for me, at this particular time, speaks to the Christ within, and inspires me to mother-forth this inner Christ; to bring my deepest Self to birth in the "redness" of daily activity.

NOTES

1 Jean Leclercq, *The Love of Learning and the Desire for God* (New York: Fordham University Press/Mentor Omega, 1961) 78.
2 Cf ibid 79.
3 St John of the Cross, 'The Living Flame of Love' in K. Kavanaugh & O. Rodriguez eds., *The Collected Works of St John of the Cross*, stanza 1.
4 From *On the Way to the Wedding* by Linda Schierse Leonard, © 1986. Reprinted by arrangement with Shambhala Productions, Inc., Boston. 217.
5 St Bernard of Clairvaux, *On the Song of Songs*, sermon 74:6f.
6 From *On the Way to the Wedding* by Linda Schierse Leonard, © 1986. Reprinted by arrangement with Shambhala Productions, Inc., Boston. 194.

Chapter 13

A Privileged Way:
The Spiritual Exercises

Experience has taught me that the privileged way of discerning "personal vocation" is through the actual making of the Ignatian Spiritual Exercises.

Herbert Alphonso S.J., *The Personal Vocation*

The Spiritual Exercises of St Ignatius of Loyola are described, by Herbert Alphonso, as the privileged way of discerning our *personal vocation*. The goal of the *Exercises* is *Election*; i.e. "God's will in the arrangement or ordering or orientation of my life for salvation."[1] As noted in Part One, God's will for me is, in its deepest sense, "my unrepeatable uniqueness, the 'name' by which God calls me – that is, my truest or deepest 'self'..."[2] Alphonso describes the movement of the Exercises as a "progressive dynamic of deepening inner freedom".[3] As the individual grows in inner freedom, he or she becomes more and more open to the positive and fruitful touch of God's Spirit, and more aware of the counter-spirits, or the negative forces, at work in the psyche.

The *Exercises* are a privileged way but they are by no means the exclusive way of discovering our God-given identity. Additionally, the Exercises are a dynamic process and the discernment of *personal vocation* will depend on how the individual has entered and stayed within the dynamic. The guidance of a wise director is also vital if the individual is to stay with his or her real experience rather than technique or mere external dogma.

With an individual's real experience in mind, it is interesting to take a brief look at the Exercises from a Jungian perspective.

159

Background History

Jung notes that while *The Spiritual Exercises* of St Ignatius of Loyola were written as late as the sixteenth century, a long religious and philosophical history precedes them. He points out that there are traces in all primitive religions of the attempt to effect a transformation in the human psyche. Traces of such attempts can be seen, he maintains, in the early days of Christian spirituality, but no system or method was developed until the Middle Ages.

The term "spiritual exercises", he remarks, appeared in the thirteenth century, and, in the fourteenth century, text books were produced with prescribed steps for meditation. The aim of these disciplined exercises was the development of human consciousness until it reached perfection in the Divinity. The end of the fourteenth century witnessed the development of the *Devotio Moderna*, an influential movement founded by Geert Groote. This movement has its classical representation in *The Imitation of Christ*, a work generally attributed to Thomas à Kempis. The Devoti drew up and offered detailed guidelines for meditation, and they endeavoured to develop deep inner piety and a life of asceticism.

Cisneros, who was a reforming abbot at Montserrat, near Barcelona in Spain, was influenced by the *Devotio Moderna* movement. Cisneros wrote a book called *Ejercitatorio della vida espiritual*, which is based on the classical three ways in Christian spirituality: i.e. the purgative way, the illuminative way and the unitive way. Don Inigo (i.e. Ignatius of Loyola) was to become the pupil of Cisneros, and Jung maintains that Cisneros' book had an influence on Ignatius. Jung holds, however, that technique has replaced individual experience in Cisneros' exercises. These exercises, Jung believes, are the technically correct substitute for the individual's experience of mystical union.[4]

Jung and the Ignatian Exercises

Jung seems to have an ambiguous attitude towards the Ignatian Exercises: they are both praised and criticised by him.

Jung points out that Ignatius abandoned the earlier meditations of the Devoti. The goal of these meditations was to submerge the individual in the Divinity, but the individual stood apart from the world. The Devoti followed an inward path cut off from the "world", but the Ignatian path led outwards to find God in all things. Jung is struck by the concrete quality of Ignatian spirituality which does not take refuge in the spirit and deny the body. However, Jung maintains that Ignatius dropped almost completely the mystical content which was so important for the Devoti. Mysticism, Jung believes, was dissolved in method; and Ignatius had militarized meditation, making it a series of meditations to be accomplished within a prescribed time. Elsewhere, however, he commends the method whereby the exercitant is ploughed through and through with parallels from the life of Christ and he proclaims that the Exercises penetrate the depths of human nature.[5]

The Exercises in Practice

The Ignatian 30-day retreat and the "19th Annotation" are the two generally accepted ways of experiencing the full Spiritual Exercises.

30-day Retreat
Ignatius suggests that greater progress is made in the Exercises if the individual withdraws from friends, acquaintances and worldly cares (cf Ex: Annotation 20). He assigns a time span of four weeks which corresponds to the four parts or movements in the dynamic of the Exercises:

Principle & Foundation

Any building needs a solid foundation and our relationship with God is no different. The foundation for the entire dynamic of the Exercises is a belief in God's creative love – a belief that all of reality exists in and through God's creative love; and a belief that each one of us is uniquely created by God and personally loved by God. This principle and foundation is comparable to the development of a strong and healthy ego, and is a necessary prerequisite for entering a demanding dynamic.

Week 1. Meditations on the reality of cosmic, global and individual sin against the backdrop of God's mysterious love. This is comparable to the purgative way and the task is self-knowledge and self-acceptance. In Jungian terms we come face to face with our own shadow in the personal unconscious and with the archetypal and collective shadow.

In this Week we realize that we belong to sinful humanity and that we, as individuals, are weak and broken; that we do not always respond to God's creative love. The focus is not so much on our failures and sinfulness, but on God's forgiving love which never fails; on God's forgiving love which desires our healing and wholeness. So this Week has both a darkening (*nigredo*) and a whitening (*albedo*) realization that we are loved sinners. Because God loves us so much God invites us to deepen and share this healing, integrating love with other people, and so we are called to work for the Kingdom.

Week 2. Contemplations on the life of Christ.

In this Week of the dynamic we reflect on how Jesus worked for the Kingdom and how God's personal love for each one of us is made visible in the person of Jesus Christ. We are ploughed through and through with parallels from the life of Christ and we are challenged to follow Christ and to incarnate the love and insight we have received.

Week 3. Contemplations on the passion of Christ.

The life of Jesus takes us to his passion and crucifixion and we reflect on God's redeeming love. We, too, are invited to hold the crucifying opposites in creative tension and to die to ego control.

Week 4. Contemplations on the Resurrection and Ascension of Christ.

As Christians we believe the story did not end with Jesus' crucifixion and death. His resurrection from the dead is central to our faith. In this Week we reflect on God's radiant love and on how the energizing, resurrecting Spirit pours through his wounds.

The aim of the Exercises is to find God's love radiating in all things and through all things. It is to view reality from God's broad perspective.

Ignatius does encourage flexibility, and he states that the "Weeks" of the Exercises do not have to consist of seven or eight days. It may be necessary to lengthen or shorten the "Weeks" in accord with the journey of each individual. For example, some people may need to spend longer on First Week material, while others may need more time to contemplate the life of Christ and the demands of discipleship. While Ignatius recognises individual needs and recommends flexibility, he does advise finishing the Exercises in approximately 30 days (cf Ex: Annotation 4).

The following are some requirements for the undertaking of a 30-day retreat:

- A commitment to four or five hours in prayer each day;
- The writing of a review of each prayer period, noting the different interior movements experienced;
- Meeting with a director for a brief period on a daily basis to share your experience;
- Maintaining an atmosphere of silence.

Ignatius highlights the following desirable dispositions in the individual who is about to undertake the Exercises:

- Generosity toward God the Creator;
- The desire to do God's will, or, in other words, the desire to be who God wants me to be, i.e. my deepest and truest Self.

Not every retreat house offers a 30-day retreat but most retreat houses could advise where to apply. Those centres which do offer such a retreat usually request a lengthy application form and some personal background information. Attendance for an interview may also be requested before being accepted.

A 30-day retreat is a *privileged* way of discerning *personal vocation* since it can be difficult to find 30+ days away from the demands of work and perhaps family. I say 30+ days as there may be some orientation time at the beginning of the retreat, and a few reflective and re-entry days at the end. It is privileged *Sabbath time.*

The 19th Annotation

In the Annotations to the Exercises, Ignatius makes provision for the person who is a suitable candidate, but is unable to enter a 30-day retreat because of the demands of work or other commitments. The 19th Annotation allows for adaptation whereby the individual can experience the Exercises during the daily routine of his or her life. Instead of withdrawing for 30 days the individual makes space for *Sabbath time* among the bits and pieces of everyday living. This *Sabbath time* takes the shape of a daily prayer period and a review of the time spent in prayer. The length of the daily prayer period may stretch from half-an-hour to one-and-a half-hours depending on the individual's circumstances. The individual writes a review of each prayer period and meets with a director once a week. When the individual receives the graces prayed for, he or she moves through the dynamic of the Exercises. This movement through the entire dynamic will take at least 30 weeks and perhaps much longer depending on each person's unique journey.

Dynamic and Desire

The dynamic of the Exercises is built on the *id quod volo*, i.e. the grace desired. The ultimate desire is for growing inner freedom and an openness to God, i.e. Truth and Love. It is a desire for inner spaciousness, a desire to view reality from God's broad perspective.

A sense of God's broad perspective is accompanied by feelings of shame and confusion: the shame and confusion felt when we realize that we are sinners unconditionally loved; sinners who have missed the mark of love and truth yet are still held, still loved, still desired; sinners who have missed the mark of our deepest identity yet are still called into being.

Patterns of "missing the mark" will emerge from a general review of our life story with its stepping stones and milestones. As we journey through life with Christ in the succeeding contemplations, there is a deepening realization of how Christ has been the cornerstone, holding the curving patterns of our life together in unity. There may be a glimpse of a white stone with our God-given name and deepest identity engraved on it. We may even hear the whisper of God calling us by name in the silent depths of our heart. It is a call which will lead us to the wounds of crucifixion and death, but, ultimately, to the spaciousness of new life.

Summary

The Spiritual Exercises of St Ignatius of Loyola are privileged *Sabbath time*. They are also a privileged but not exclusive way of discerning *personal vocation* which is written into our concrete history. The Exercises take the field of our life and turn it over to God. They plough the individual through and through with parallels from the life of Christ and they penetrate the depths of human nature.

Desire is central to the dynamic movement of the Exercises and when the plough meets with obstacles in the field of our lives, we are encouraged to pray for the desire to desire:

In the depths of my being you are my God,
at the rising of the sun I seek your face.
My heart thirsts for you, my flesh longs for you,
in a barren and dry land where no water is.

I search for you in unexpected places,
at the edges of the known, in the language of dreams,
in the wilderness of the city streets,
in the grim towers where the desperate dwell.

There may I look long and lovingly,
there may I listen for the word beyond words,
there may I wait for a glimpse of your glory,
there may I utter strange songs of your praise...

With manna in my exile do you feed me,
with water springing up from parched land.
I am deeply satisfied with a sumptuous feast,
my whole being resounds with murmurs of joy...

I hear your voice, Do not be afraid.
You sustain me in the watches of the night,
your hovering wings give me shade on my journey.
I stumble, yet I trust you not to let go.

The faces of terror will prove my friends yet,
guarding as they do my fragile soul-self,

waiting the calm word of the approach of true love,
waiting to be named as faithful and true.

So shall I emerge to the place of rejoicing,
the child and the adult linked arm in arm.
We shall see your face in all your creatures,
we shall know the truth in our hearts.[6]

NOTES

1   Herbert Alphonso, op. cit., 19/20.
2   ibid 20.
3   ibid 46/47.
4   Cf Barbara Hannah, ed., *Modern Psychology Volume 3 & 4*, Notes on
     lectures given at the Eidgenossische Technische Hochschule, Zurich, by
     Prof. C. G. Jung, October 1938-March 1940.
5   Cf ibid.
6   Jim Cotter, Psalm 63, Stanzas 1-3; 6; 9-11 in *By Stony Paths, A Version of
     Psalms 51-100* (Sheffield: Cairns Pub., 1991) 25/26.

Chapter 14

Brief Exercises

...the kingdom of Heaven is close at hand.
Mt 4:17, JB trans.

The inner kingdom is deep yet close, profound yet simple. This chapter introduces a number of brief and simple exercises which may be helpful in tapping into the depth of our *personal vocation* and personal myth. They are very simple tools for divining life-giving springs and hidden treasure.

Exercise 1: "I am"

Let "I am" statements rise spontaneously to consciousness and record them.

I am ....

I am ....

I am ....

When you have recorded a fairly lengthy list of "I am" statements, read back over them and see if there are any places where you can say "I am more than......" Now, make a new list of statements.

I am more than ....

I am more than ....

I am more than ....

This exercise gets us in touch with our societal roles, persona identity and ego-ideals. It can alert us to what is transient and superficial, and to what is deep and constant. Try to deepen this awareness by working with the images of mask and flame. Draw as many masks as you want. Masks represent persona identity which is a necessary buffer for our dealings with the external world. Try to name the many masks you wear or the roles you play. These masks and roles are very important but you are more than the mask, more than the role. Take an imaginative x-ray of the masks and draw or name what lies behind them.

Draw a flame with onion-like layers. The flame represents what is deeper than persona and ego-identity, and it has different layers moving in toward the centre or essence. Fill in your depth statements here which relate to being rather than doing. The centre of the flame represents our divine spark and deepest identity.

Exercise 2: Peaks and Valleys

Draw a line of peaks and valleys, representing the high and low points in your life. Give each peak and valley a name. What is the connecting thread between the peaks? What brings you greatest joy? What is the connecting thread between the valleys? What causes you deep sorrow? What do you cling to in moments of darkness, pain or desperation? What is common to all the experiences? Is there a link between your greatest joys and your deepest sorrows?

Deepen this reflection by writing your own epitaph or obituary.

Now imagine your name written in the Book of Life by the hand of God. By what name does God call you?

Exercise 3: Spontaneous Feeling

Have you ever felt spontaneously close to God? If so, recall as many moments as possible? What is the pattern in these moments of spontaneous intimacy and union?

Are these moments connected in any way to the peaks and valleys in your life?

Exercise 4: Favourite Scripture Quotations

Look up all your favourite passages from Scripture. Is there a word, or phrase, which you find particularly striking, a word or phrase which warms and moves your heart? Is there a common thread, or theme, or word, in the passages which you have chosen, perhaps?

How does this word of Scripture compare with the epitaph or obituary you have written? Does your favourite word from Scripture resonate with your name in the Book of Life?

Exercise 5: At Home

Imagine yourself as a house which is your home. Draw a house which represents you as a person. Is there any part of the house in which you feel most at home? Is there any part you do not like? Are some quarters in need of repair or in danger of neglect?

Do you feel the need to build on an extension?

What are the foundations like? Have you got a sense of a cornerstone? Can you name the cornerstone which is holding the whole structure together?

Design a coat of arms for this special house and write its particular motto.

Exercise 6: A Letter

In 2 Corinthians 3:3, St Paul states that,
    ...you are a letter of Christ...written not with ink but

with the Spirit of the living God, not on tablets of stone but on tablets of human hearts.

Try to get a sense of Christ writing a letter on your heart. Wait with eagerness for the delivery or arrival of this letter. Imagine the letter Christ has addressed to you and write it out. Christ has a special name for you - a kind of pet name. What does he call you? What does he say?

This letter of Christ comes to us every day in ever-deepening shades of light and understanding. It is a letter written on our hearts and, therefore, on our whole personality. It is a letter which is always growing and expanding, drawing us into the depths of our being and beyond. It is a long, deep story.

Chapter 15

Logos and Eros:
A General Summary

*"...my name is growing all the time, and I've lived a very
long, long time; so my name is like a story. Real names tell
you the story of the things they belong to in my language..."*
J.R.R. Tolkien, *The Lord of the Rings*

Real names tell us the story of their being and of what they
belong to in the Old Speech and language.

Names emanate from the *Logos*, or Word, which is the
discriminating, dividing masculine principle. The masculine
Logos principle separates and distinguishes. It enables us to
recognise individuality and uniqueness.

Eros, on the other hand, is the archetype of relationship.
It is the feminine *Eros* principle that binds and attracts. It
enables us to experience interconnectedness and unity.

Real names are born of the interplay between the
masculine and feminine energies. Real names distinguish us
as unique individuals and they tell the story of the things to
which we belong. They tell the story both of our individuality and of our relatedness.

The God who calls us by name has both masculine and
feminine qualities. She-He enfolds us in womb-like darkness and, simultaneously, leads us into the differentiating
light. Our God sets us apart as individuals from the crowd
and, at once, draws us into involvement, interconnectedness
and personal relationship. Our *personal vocation* differentiates
us as being unique and holds us in a personal bond.

In the Book of Deuteronomy God is portrayed in both
masculine and feminine imagery as the Rock who bore us
and the God who gave us birth (cf Dt 32:18). God's active

and receptive energies of the masculine and the feminine
are also seen in the Book of Isaiah:

> Listen to me, O house of Jacob,
>> all the remnant of the house of Israel,
>> who have been borne by me
>>> from your birth,
>> carried from the womb;
> even to your old age I am he,
>> even when you turn grey I will carry you.
> I have made and I will bear;
>> I will carry and will save (Is 46:3,4).

This image of a pregnant God is also present in the Book of
Isaiah where God cries out like a woman in labour, gasping
and panting (cf Is 42:14); and where God promises not to
forget her nursing child, the child of her womb (cf Is
49:15). The bonding feminine principle is also seen in the
image of God as a knitter, weaving and knitting us together
in the maternal womb (cf Ps 139:13).

It is the interplay between the feminine and the masculine energies of God which binds us to God's very own self
and inscribes our individual name on the palm of God's
very own hands (cf Is 49:16). And it is the complementary
energies of the masculine and the feminine, of the active
and the receptive, which makes our God such a creative
storyteller. God, our storyteller, spins a web of darkness and
of light; a web of distinct shapes and of merging shadows; a
web of separateness and of interconnectedness; a web of
feasting and of fasting; a web of absence and of presence; a
web of immanence and of transcendence.

In calling us by name God writes the essence of our
unfolding and never ending story. Our name and our story
is growing all the time since we are born of the eternal
Word or *Logos* who binds us with feminine wisdom to the
creative breast of God (cf Jn 1:18).

In the Incarnation the eternal *Logos* becomes the feminine earthy principle of flesh (cf Jn 1:14), and the union of the masculine and feminine principles is actual. Christ Jesus is both Father-*Logos*-spirit-sky and Mother-*Eros*-flesh-earth.

Christ Jesus, too, is both the masculine Word of God and the feminine Wisdom of God. The crucified Christ who holds all opposites in creative tension is identified with the feminine *Sophia* by St Paul: "...we proclaim Christ crucified, a stumbling block to Jews and foolishness to Gentiles, but to those who are the called, both Jews and Greeks, Christ the power of God and the wisdom of God" (1 Cor 1:24). The Word or *Logos* is impersonal, objective knowledge while Wisdom, or *Sophia*, is personal, subjective knowledge. *Sophia* is another aspect of the feminine bonding principle. The Word is *Sophia* and *Sophia* is the Word.

In the Book of Proverbs Wisdom has built her house (cf Pr 9:1) and in St John's gospel Jesus states: "If you make my word your home you will indeed be my disciples..." (Jn 8:31; JB trans.) Wisdom has mixed her wine and set her table and she offers the invitation:

> Come, eat of my bread
>   and drink of the wine I have mixed.
> Lay aside immaturity, and live,
>   and walk in the way of insight (Pr 9:5,6).

And in St John's gospel Jesus proclaims that he is the bread of life:

> Jesus said to them, "I am the bread of life. Whoever comes to me will never be hungry, and whoever believes in me will never be thirsty" (Jn 6:35).

Eugene Pascal points out that our initial experiences of the feminine principle of relatedness, such as the gestation period in the dark and nurturing womb, and enfoldment and suckling at the mother's breast, produce "in later life such erotic (the adjective that derives from *Eros*) things as the phenomenon of food sharing, the ritual of communion and solidarity among those at table."[1] This feminine erotic principle is evident in Jesus' invitation to eat his flesh and drink his blood. This is his promise: "Those who eat my flesh and drink my blood abide in me, and I in them" (Jn 6:56). This is the erotic desire of the God who carves our name on divine flesh. This is the erotic desire of the God who calls us into individuality so that we can truly be united. This is the invitation to the erotic wedding banquet: the wedding of the masculine and the feminine; of the human and divine; of heaven and earth; of time and eternity. This is the invitation to be fertile and to give birth to the Self.

We are made in the image and likeness of God who transcends gender but is a dynamic movement of masculine and feminine energies. Giving birth to the Self is an ongoing process, and our *personal vocation* and personal myth are growing all the time through the interplay of masculine and feminine energies. These energies draw us ever deeper into our own individuality and uniqueness, and into relationship with others, the world and God.

Our story is a long, long story. It reaches back to the eternal Word and Wisdom of God; it is written on the stones of the earth and on the hands of time; it unfolds into eternity and is held by God.

The principles of the differentiating masculine *Logos* and the bonding feminine *Eros* are at work in this attempted synthesis of Alphonso's *Personal vocation* and Jung's *Personal Myth*. In attempting a synthesis it is important to see psychology and spirituality as two distinct disciplines but as two distinct disciplines which are interrelated. The danger of psychologizing spirituality and of spiritualizing psychology must be avoided. Reductionism leads to a zone of entrapment. Additionally, the demonization of psychology, which seems to occur in some Christian circles, cuts one off from humanity and the human journey. It fails to honour incarnation and creation. On the other hand, the dismissal of spirituality and genuine religion leaves one merely in the human. It fails to open the way to transcendent divine love.

Our personal *myth* is the call to become a unique individual, the best human being possible. Our *personal vocation* embraces this call but takes us a step deeper. It recognizes that we are called by name into unique individuality by the transcendent God made manifest in Christ Jesus. Our *personal vocation* is the unique encounter of our incomparable individuality with the transcendent God. Our *personal vocation* is a window into the prismatic cosmic Christ; a window onto the transcendent reality of the Trinity.

A synthesis of Jung's *Personal Myth* and Alphonso's *Personal Vocation* has, I believe, an invaluable contribution to make to a Christian model of psycho-spiritual development and transformation. The individuation process, which involves a death-like experience to ego-control and the relativization of the ego to a greater Centre, is in keeping with Christ's saying: "Those who find their life will lose it, and those who lose their life for my sake will find it" (Mt 10:39). Additionally, the communal aspect which is so important for Christian spirituality is also reflected in the psychological process of individuation. As John Welch O.Carm. states:

> The individuation process is not a narcissistic trip. It is actually a journey into community. Ego-consciousness is actually the isolated existence as it struggles for identity and control. Movement toward the Self is a movement into a common life. The deeper down the psyche I descend, the less I am "I" and the more I am "we".[2]

Even though Alphonso, in his treatment of *Personal Vocation*, appears to take the Trinitarian dimension somewhat for granted, his spirituality is Trinitarian as well as being very Christocentric. *Christ*, the Word made flesh, is the unique mediator between the *Father* (Mother) and humankind who incarnates in us through the *Spirit*. The Trinity in

Jung's thought, however, does present difficulty for a Christian spirituality. The introduction of Satan into the Trinity in order to make up a quaternity is theologically unacceptable. Ann B. Ulanov offers a suggestion which would surmount the Trinity-Quaternity problem: "Are we humans the four-cornered base of the pyramid of the Trinity, that which earths it, thus making us participate in the ongoing eternal incarnation?"[3] Meanwhile the problem of God's "dark side" and the question of evil remains. A treatment of the problem is beyond the scope of this work, yet it is important to raise it since it is an uncomfortable challenge to spiritual theology and Trinitarian thought.

What is clear is that our own Shadow projections as individuals and as nations can lead to evil behaviours such as racial prejudice, sectarianism, war and intolerance of all kinds. Growth in freedom, responsibility and love involves the withdrawal of projections from other people and also from God. It requires an ever-increasing consciousness of what is in the hidden folds of the heart or the unconscious. Jung's analytical psychology has much to offer in the area of spiritual discernment as it can illuminate shadow projections and areas of self deception. On the other hand, the Ignatian rules for discernment complement Jung's lack of guidance for discriminating between negative or evil forces as they operate in the psyche. The discernment of our *personal vocation* is the ultimate protection from evil since our real name comes from the depths where only God abides. In speaking of individuation and the white stone with a new name, Jeanne Heiberg states:

>...The stone is also a symbol of protection. In the time when Revelation was written, it was a pagan custom to wear an amulet, a stone or other object worn around the neck for protection from evil. A name that no one else was allowed to know was written on the amulet... The angel's promise of a white stone with a secret name meant not only

individuation and transformation in God but also protection from evil.[4]

In addition, our *personal vocation*, which is a maturing inter-personal love relationship between us and the person of Christ Jesus, offers the necessary support for the ongoing dynamic process of individuation. It is important to remember that our *personal myth* and *personal vocation* are descriptive of an ever deepening, spiralling movement which takes the individual deeper and deeper into the recesses of the psyche and beyond, where the spirit of God sweeps over the face of the unconscious (cf Gen 1:2) and blows where it chooses (cf Jn 3:8).

This ongoing dynamic process, which unfolds new aspects of our deepest and truest Self, involves an encounter with woundedness and danger. This is evident from the Scriptural background of vocation and from the work of Carl Jung. This wounding and danger may be experienced interiorly and exteriorly. The ego's encounter with forces beyond its control is fraught with danger and its relativization to a greater Centre is experienced as a wounding. The call to incarnate our uniqueness in daily living runs the risk of conflict with external authority and the wound of punishment from this authority and from the collective. However, it is through this woundedness that divine life and energy ultimately flow.

The inner wounding is a symbolic incestuous act which leads to inner marriage and spiritual union. The engagement in this symbolic incest is necessary to experience the energies of love within. This healthy energy can then be directed towards others and God. When we meditate and contemplate we are involved in sacred incest: we are becoming one with our deepest Self and are tending the divine spark within. It is this incestuous act which opens us up at the core of our being and empowers us to live the Lord's triple command to love self, neighbour and God.

Sabbath time creates space for this sacred intrapenetration which deepens the quality of our inner and outer relatedness.

Average healthy living involves balancing activity and rest i.e. the active masculine energies and the feminine receptive energies. In *Sabbath time* we rest from the daily external activities, which we call work, and we are recharged physically and mentally. Truly wholesome living will renew us body, soul and spirit. To live a truly wholesome life we need to spend some *Sabbath time* listening to the wisdom of the body, and attending to soul-shaping and the divine fire within. This quality *Sabbath time* is sacred space for our core creative Self and for our God, and is essential if our inner land is to have its wedding and remain fertile:

> The Lord spoke to Moses on Mount Sinai, saying: "Speak to the people of Israel and say to them: 'When you enter the land that I am giving you, the land shall observe a Sabbath for the Lord. Six years you shall sow your field, and six years you shall prune your vineyard, and gather in their yield; but in the seventh year there shall be a Sabbath of complete rest for the land, a Sabbath for the Lord: you shall not sow your field or prune your vineyard. You shall not reap the aftergrowth of your harvest or gather the grapes of your unpruned vine: it shall be a year of complete rest for the land. You may eat what the land yields during its Sabbath – you, your male and female slaves, your hired and your bound labourers who live with you; for your livestock also, and for the wild animals in your land all its yield shall be for food'" (Lev 25: 1-6).

This fallow period is necessary for the ongoing work of the plough and of the seed. It is a time, for the land, of deep deep nourishment not visible to the naked eye. It is a time of deep nourishment for every aspect of our inner land – for the masculine and the feminine; for the free and the bound; for the wild and the tame.

Each individual must discover his or her own rhythm and pattern of *Sabbath time*. Ideally, this pattern unfolds on a daily, weekly, monthly and seasonal basis, and culminates every seventh year in a "big" *Sabbath*. The keeping of these *Sabbath times* helps us to discover our God-given inner path and to remain on it.

There is no prescriptive answer to the quest for one's unique, God-given pathway in life. There are opportunities for *Sabbath time*: *Sabbath time* which allows our core creative and deepest Self to express itself; *Sabbath time* which allows the sand of our lives to become the white stone which ignites the divine spark that transforms to living bone.

The expression of our core creative and deepest Self may take various shapes. It may take the shape of a painting. It may visit us by the wings of dreams or through the open door of a wound. It may ache to take the shape of a word on paper. It may transpose itself into music or song or dance. It may rise as a whispered voice during meditation or contemplation.

We are called. We are called by name to be our deepest and truest Self and to give expression to this Self. This *personal vocation* is a God-given prayer written on the pages of our personal story. We are a prayer. At our deepest Centre there is pure desire and when we live from the truth of this Centre we are a living prayer. So, let us be our deepest and truest Self. Let us hear our own story. Let us live our own life-script.

NOTES

1 Eugene Pascal, *Jung to Live By* (London: Souvenir Press, 1994) 148.
2 John Welch O.Carm., op.cit., 105.
3 Ann Belford Ulanov, op. cit., 98.
4 Jeanne Heiberg, *Winning Your Inner Battle* (California: Resource Pub., 1989) 107.

SUGGESTED READING

Alphonso, Herbert, *The Personal Vocation*, Gujarat, India: Prakash, 1991.

Avis, Paul, *Eros and the Sacred*, London: SPCK, 1989.

Bausch, William J., *Storytelling Imagination and Faith,* Mystic, Connecticut: Twenty-Third Pub., (1984) 1988.

Boff, Leonardo, *Liberating Grace*, New York: Maryknoll, 1979.

Bosnak, Robert, *A Little Course in Dreams*, Boston & Shaftesbury: Shambhala, 1988.

Carretto, Carlo, *The God Who Comes*, London: Darton, Longman & Todd, 1974.

Cassirer, Ernst, *The Philosophy of Symbolic Forms*, New Haven: Yale University Press, 1953-7.

Chetwynd, Tom, *A Dictionary of Symbols*, London: Paladin/Collins, 1982.

Coxhead, D., & Hiller, S., *Dreams*, London: Thames and Hudson, (1976) 1990.

Cunningham, A., Jungian Psychology: Its Contribution to Spirituality in Richardson, A., & Bowden, J., eds., *A New Dictionary of Christian Theology*, London: SCM Press, 1983.

Denny, Frederick, Names and Naming in Eliade, M., ed., T*he Encyclopaedia of Religion Vol 10*, New York: Macmillan Pub. Co., 1987.

Dourley, John P., *The Illness That We Are: A Jungian Critique of Christianity,* Toronto: Inner City Books, 1984.

Dourley, John P., Love, *Celibacy and the Inner Marriage*, Toronto: Inner City Books, 1987.

Doyle, Brendan, *Meditations with Julian of Norwich*, Santa Fe, New Mexico: Bear & Co., 1983.

de Verteuil, Michel, *Your Word is a Light for my Steps*: *Lectio Divina*, Dublin: Veritas, 1996.

Edinger, Edward F., *The Bible and the Psyche: Individuation Symbolism in the Old Testament*, Toronto: Inner City Books, 1986.

Edinger, Edward F., *The Mysterium Lectures: A Journey through C. G. Jung's Mysterium Coniunctionis*, Toronto: Inner City Books, 1995.

Egan, Harvey D., Ignatian Spirituality in Downey, Michael, ed., *The New Dictionary of Catholic Spirituality*, Collegeville, Minnesota: The Liturgical Press, 1993.

Eliade, Mircea, *The Sacred and the Profane: The Nature of Religion*, New York: Harcourt Brace & World Inc., 1959.

Ferder, Fran, *Words Made Flesh: Scripture, Psychology and Human Communication*, Notre Dame, Indiana: Ave Maria Press, 1986.

Giegerich, Wolfgang, The Advent of the Guest: Shadow Integration and the Rise of Psychology in Hillman, James et al., eds., *Spring 51 A Journal of Archetype and Culture*, Dallas, Texas: Spring Pub., 1991.

Goldbrunner, Josef, *Individuation: A Study of the Depth-Psychology of Jung*, London: Hollis & Carter, 1955.

Grant, W.H., et al., *From Image to Likeness: A Jungian Path in the Gospel Journey*, New York: Paulist Press, 1983.

Hannah, B. ed., *Modern Psychology Vol. 3 & 4*, Notes on Lectures given at the Eidgenossische Technische Hochschule, Zurich, by Prof. C. G. Jung, October 1938-March 1940.

Harding, Esther, What makes the Symbol effective as a healing agent? in Adler, G., ed., *Current Trends in Analytical Psychology*, London: Tavistock Pub., 1961.

Heiberg, Jeanne, *Winning Your Inner Battle*, San Jose, California: Resource Pub., 1989.

Heisig, James W., *Imago Dei: A Study of C. G. Jung's Psychology of Religion*, Lewisburg: Bucknell University Press, 1979.

Hostie, Raymond, *Religion and the Psychology of Jung*, London/New York: Sheed & Ward, 1957.

Huebsch, Bill, *A Spirituality of Wholeness: The New Look at Grace,* Mystic, Connecticut: Twenty-Third Pub., 1988.

Jacobi, Jolande, *Complex, Archetype, Symbol in the Psychology of C. G. Jung*, New York: Princeton University Press, (1959) 1974.

Jaffé, Aniela, *Was C. G. Jung a Mystic? And Other Essays*, Einsiedeln, Switzerland: Daimon Verlag, 1989.

Jaffe, Lawrence, *Liberating the Heart*, Toronto: Inner City Books, 1990.

Johnson, Robert A., *Ecstasy: Understanding the Psychology of Joy*, San Francisco: Harper & Row, 1987.

Johnson, Robert A., *We: Understanding the Psychology of Romantic Love*, San Francisco: Harper & Row, 1983.

Johnson, Robert A., *Inner Work*, New York: HarperCollins/ HarperSanFrancisco, (1986) 1989.

Johnston, William, S.J., *The Mirror Mind*, New York: Fordham University Press, 1981.

Jung, Albert, Self-Realization in Adler, G., ed., *Current Trends in Analytical Psychology*, London: Tavistock Pub., 1961.

Jung, C. G., *Psychological Types CW VI*, London: Routledge & Kegan Paul, 1971.

Jung, C. G., *Two Essays on Analytical Psychology CW VII*, London: Routledge & Kegan Paul, 1953.

Jung, C. G., *The Archetypes and the Collective Unconscious CW IX, I*, London: Routledge & Kegan Paul, (1959) 1969.

Jung, C. G., *Aion: Researches into the Phenomenology of the Self CW IX, II*, London: Routledge & Kegan Paul, (1959) 1968.

Jung, C. G., *Civilization in Transition CW X*, London: Routledge & Kegan Paul, 1964.

Jung, C. G., *Psychology and Alchemy CW XII*, London: Routledge & Kegan Paul, 1953.

Jung, C. G., *Mysterium Coniunctionis CW XIV*, London: Routledge & Kegan Paul, (1963) 1970.

Jung, C. G., *The Practice of Psychotherapy CW XVI*, London: Routledge & Kegan Paul, (1954) 1976.

Jung, C. G., *Modern Man in Search of A Soul*, London: Routledge & Kegan Paul, (1933) 1961.

Jung, C. G., *Psychology and Religion*, New Haven: Yale University Press, (1938) 1964.

Jung, C. G., *Answer to Job*, London: Routledge & Kegan Paul, 1954.

Jung, C. G., *Analytical Psychology: Its Theory and Practice*, London: Ark/Routledge, (1986) 1990.

Jung, C. G., *Memories, Dreams, Reflections*, New York: Vintage Books, 1965.

Jung, C. G., *The Integration of the Personality*, London: Routledge & Kegan Paul, (1940) 1963.

Jung, C. G., ed., *Man and his Symbols*, London: Picador/Pan, 1978.

Jung, C. G., & Kerenyi, C., *Essays on a Science of Mythology*, New Jersey: Princeton University Press, (1969) 1973.

Keirsey, D., & Bates, M., *Please Understand Me: Character & Temperament Types*, Del Mar, CA: Prometheus Nemesis Book Co., 1984.

Kelsey, Morton, *Transcend*, New York: Crossroad, 1985.

Kelsey, Morton & Barbara, *Sacrament of Sexuality: The Spirituality and Psychology of Sex*, Rockport, MA/Shaftesbury, Dorset: Element, 1986 & 1991.

Leclercq, Jean, *The Love of Learning and the Desire for God*, New York: Fordham University Press, 1961.

Leonard, Linda S., *The Wounded Woman: Healing the Father-Daughter Relationship*, Boston: Shambhala, 1985.

Leonard, Linda S., *On the Way to the Wedding*, Boston: Shambhala, 1987.

Lonsdale, David, *Eyes To See, Ears To Hear: An Introduction to Ignatian Spirituality*, London: Darton, Longman & Todd, 1990.

Main, John, *The Inner Christ*, London: Darton, Longman & Todd, 1987.

Meehan, Bridget M., *Delighting in the Feminine Divine*, Kansas: Sheed & Ward, 1994.

Metz, Johannes, *Poverty of Spirit*, New York/Mahwah: Paulist Press, 1968.

Moore, R. L., ed., *Carl Jung and Christian Spirituality*, New York/Mahwah: Paulist Press, 1988.

Moseley, R. M., *Becoming a Self before God*, Nashville: Abingdon Press, 1991.

McGann, Diarmuid, *Journeying within Transcendence: The Gospel of John through a Jungian Perspective*, London: Collins, 1989.

Neumann, Erich, *Amor and Psyche: The Psychic Development of the Feminine*, Princeton: Princeton University Press, (1971) 1990.

Nouwen, Henri, *Reaching Out*, London: Harper Collins, 1976.

O'Mahony, G., *Finding the Still Point*, Guildford, Surrey: Eagle, 1993.

Pascal, Eugene, *Jung to Live By*, London: Souvenir Press, 1994.

Perkins, John, *The Forbidden Self*, Boston: Shambhala, 1992.

Progoff, Ira, *At a Journal Workshop*, New York: Dialogue House, 1975.

Progoff, Ira, *The Star/Cross: An Entrance Meditation*, New York: Dialogue House, (1971) 1981.

Progoff, Ira, *The Well and The Cathedral: An Entrance Meditation*, New York: Dialogue House, (1971) 1977.

Progoff, Ira, *The White Robed Monk: An Entrance Meditation*, New York: Dialogue House, (1972) 1979.

Puhl, Louis, *The Spiritual Exercises of St Ignatius*, Chicago: University Press, 1951.

Rieff, Philip, *The Triumph of the Therapeutic*, London: Chatto & Windus, 1966.

Rollins, Wayne, *Jung and the Bible*, Atlanta: John Knox Press, 1983.

Sanford, John A., *Evil: The Shadow Side of Reality*, New York: Crossroad, 1981.

Sanford, John A., *Healing and Wholeness*, New York: Paulist Press, 1977.

Sanford, John A., *The Invisible Partners*, New York: Paulist Press, 1980.

Sanford, John A., *Mystical Christianity: A Psychological Commentary on the Gospel of John*, New York: Crossroad, 1995.

Schaer, Hans, *Religion and the Cure of Souls in Jung's Psychology*, London: Routledge & Kegan Paul, 1951.

Singer, June, *Love's Energies*, Boston: Sigo Press, 1990.

Stevens, Anthony, *On Jung*, London: Routledge, 1990.

Taylor, Jeremy, *Dream Work: Techniques for Discovering the Creative Power in Dreams*, New York/Ramsey: Paulist Press, 1983.

Ulanov, Ann B., *The Wisdom of the Psyche*, Cambridge, Mass.: Cowley Pub., 1988.

von der Heydt, Vera, *Prospects for the Soul: Soundings in Jungian Psychology and Religion*, London: Darton, Longman & Todd, 1976.

Welch, John, *Spiritual Pilgrims: Carl Jung and Teresa of Avila*, New York: Paulist Press, 1982.

Westman, Heinz, *The Springs of Creativity: The Bible and the Creative Process of the Psyche*, Wilmette, Illinois: Chiron Pub., 1986.

Westman, Heinz, *The Structure of Biblical Myths: The Ontogenesis of the Psyche*, Wilmette, Illinois: Chiron Pub., 1991.

Whitmont, Edward C., *The Symbolic Quest: Basic concepts of Analytical Psychology*, New Jersey: Princeton University Press, (1969) 1991.

Woodman, Marion, *The Ravaged Bridegroom: Masculinity in Women*, Toronto: Inner city Books, 1990.

Novels

Hardy, Thomas, *Tess of the d'Urbervilles*, London: Macmillan, 1975.

Le Guin, Ursula, *A Wizard of Earthsea*, Middlesex: Penguin/ Puffin, (1971) 1986.